Table of Contents:

1. **Introduction to Leveraged Buyouts (LBOs)**
   - Definition and Basics
   - Advantages and Risks
2. **Mindset and Preparation**
   - Developing the Right Mindset
   - Understanding Risk and Reward
   - Assessing Personal and Financial Readiness
3. **Setting Acquisition Criteria**
   - Identifying Target Industries
   - Defining Company Size and Financial Metrics
   - Geographic Considerations
4. **Deal Sourcing Strategies**
   - Leveraging Virtual Assistants
   - Networking and Industry Connections
   - Using Online Platforms and Resources
5. **Communicating with Sellers**
   - Crafting Persuasive Letters and Emails
   - Establishing Trust and Credibility
   - Emphasizing Safety and Stability
6. **Best Sectors to Target**
   - Analyzing Industry Trends and Opportunities
   - Evaluating Growth Potential and Stability
   - Assessing Competitive Landscape
7. **Understanding Valuation Methods**
   - Discounted Cash Flow (DCF) Analysis
   - EBITDA and Free Cash Flow (FCF) Multiples
   - Comparables and Market Analysis
8. **Negotiating the Deal**
   - Strategies for Win-Win Negotiations
   - Balancing Price, Terms, and Conditions
   - Handling Counteroffers and Objections
9. **Deal Structure and Financing**
   - Exploring Different Financing Options
     - Asset-Based Lending
     - Invoice Financing
     - Merchant Financing
   - Leveraging Target Company Assets and Cash Reserves
10. **Positioning Yourself as a Buyer**

- Building a Strong Personal Brand
- Demonstrating Expertise and Experience
- Creating a Professional Image
11. **Heads of Terms/LOI**
    - Understanding Key Terms and Conditions
    - Drafting Comprehensive Letters of Intent
12. **Due Diligence Process**
    - Conducting Thorough Financial Analysis
    - Assessing Legal, Regulatory, and Compliance Issues
    - Evaluating Operational and Strategic Fit
13. **Contract Negotiation and Drafting**
    - Working with Legal Professionals
    - Ensuring Clarity and Legal Compliance
14. **Closing the Deal**
    - Finalizing Legal and Financial Documents
    - Celebrating Successful Completion
15. **Post-Acquisition Management**
    - The First 90 Days: Integration and Transition
    - Implementing Growth Strategies
    - Monitoring Performance and Adjusting Strategies
16. **Special Purpose Vehicles (SPVs)**
    - Understanding the Purpose and Structure
    - Benefits and Considerations
17. **Data Rooms and Documentation**
    - Setting Up and Managing Data Rooms
    - Organizing and Securing Documentation
18. **Additional Considerations**
    - Tax Implications and Strategies
    - Regulatory Compliance
    - Risk Management
19. **Conclusion**
    - Recap of Key Concepts and Strategies
    - Looking Ahead to Future Opportunities
20. **Partner with Epitome capital and leverage our resources**

Chapter 1: Introduction to Leveraged Buyouts (LBOs)
Definition and Basics
What is a Leveraged Buyout (LBO)?

A Leveraged Buyout (LBO) is a sophisticated financial strategy used by companies or private equity firms to acquire another company by primarily using borrowed funds. The acquisition is characterized by high leverage, meaning the majority of the purchase price is funded through debt, while a smaller portion is financed with equity from the buyer.

In an LBO, the acquired company's assets and cash flows are often used as collateral for the loans needed to finance the acquisition. This enables the buyer to control a significant business entity with a relatively small upfront investment, leveraging the target company's value to secure the necessary financing.

Key Components of an LBO

1. **Target Company**: The selection of the target company is a critical step in the LBO process. Ideal targets typically have stable and predictable cash flows, strong market positions, undervalued assets, and potential for operational improvements. These characteristics ensure that the company can generate sufficient cash flow to service the debt incurred during the acquisition.
2. **Equity Investment**: This is the portion of the purchase price funded by the buyer's own capital. Although it constitutes a smaller fraction compared to the debt, the equity investment represents the buyer's stake in the company. The lower the equity investment relative to the debt, the higher the potential return on equity, but this also increases the financial risk.
3. **Debt Financing**: The bulk of the financing for an LBO comes from debt. This can include various forms of debt such as senior loans, subordinated loans, mezzanine financing, and high-yield bonds. The structure and terms of the debt are critical, as they determine the financial burden on the target company and the feasibility of the buyout.

4. **Collateral**: The target company's assets, such as real estate, inventory, receivables, and sometimes even intellectual property, are used as collateral to secure the loans. This provides lenders with a degree of security in the event of default.
5. **Buyout Group**: This typically consists of private equity firms, institutional investors, or a consortium of investors. The buyout group is responsible for identifying the target, structuring the deal, securing financing, and managing the post-acquisition operations.

Basic Mechanics of an LBO

1. **Identifying the Target**: The process begins with identifying a suitable target company. This involves extensive research and analysis to find a company with the right financial and operational characteristics. Factors such as industry stability, market position, historical performance, and growth potential are considered.
2. **Structuring the Deal**: Once a target is identified, the next step is to structure the deal. This involves negotiating the purchase price, determining the mix of debt and equity, and outlining the terms of the transaction. The goal is to create a financial structure that maximizes returns while maintaining manageable risk levels.
3. **Securing Financing**: After structuring the deal, the buyer secures financing from various lenders. This involves presenting a compelling case to banks, institutional investors, and other financing sources. The financing package typically includes a mix of senior debt (which has the highest priority in case of liquidation), mezzanine debt (which is subordinate to senior debt but senior to equity), and sometimes high-yield bonds.
4. **Closing the Acquisition**: Once financing is secured, the acquisition is finalized. This includes completing legal documentation, transferring ownership, and initiating any planned changes in management or operations. The closing process can be complex and involves coordination between

multiple parties, including legal advisors, financial advisors, and regulatory bodies.
5. **Post-Acquisition Management**: After the acquisition is complete, the focus shifts to managing the target company. The new owners work to improve operational efficiencies, reduce costs, and drive revenue growth. Effective post-acquisition management is crucial for ensuring that the company can generate sufficient cash flow to service its debt and achieve the desired return on investment.

Advantages and Risks
Advantages of Leveraged Buyouts

1. **High Return on Equity (ROE)**: One of the primary attractions of LBOs is the potential for high returns on equity. By using debt to finance the majority of the acquisition, the buyer can control a large asset with a relatively small equity investment. If the target company performs well, the returns on the invested equity can be substantial. This leverage amplifies the gains for equity holders.
2. **Tax Benefits**: Interest payments on the borrowed funds used in an LBO are tax-deductible, reducing the overall tax burden for the acquired company. This tax shield effectively lowers the cost of borrowing and enhances the net cash flow available for debt servicing and reinvestment.
3. **Control and Influence**: LBOs often result in significant ownership stakes for the buyout group, granting them substantial control over the target company's operations and strategic direction. This level of influence enables the new owners to implement changes that can enhance the company's performance and value.
4. **Enhanced Efficiency**: The necessity to service a large amount of debt imposes financial discipline on the target company. This often leads to improvements in operational efficiency, cost management, and overall productivity. The pressure to optimize performance can drive significant positive changes in the company's operations.

Risks of Leveraged Buyouts

1. **High Debt Levels**: The substantial debt burden associated with LBOs can pose significant risks. If the target company's cash flows are insufficient to meet debt obligations, it may face financial distress or even bankruptcy. The high leverage ratio increases the company's financial vulnerability.
2. **Interest Rate Risk**: Changes in interest rates can significantly impact the cost of borrowing. An increase in interest rates can raise the debt servicing costs, squeezing the company's cash flow and reducing its financial flexibility. Interest rate volatility is a critical risk factor that needs to be managed.
3. **Operational Risks**: The pressure to improve operational performance and generate sufficient cash flow to service debt can be challenging. Management may face difficulties in executing strategic changes, optimizing operations, or achieving the projected financial targets. Operational disruptions can negatively impact the company's performance and its ability to meet debt obligations.
4. **Market and Economic Risks**: Economic downturns or adverse market conditions can affect the target company's revenue and profitability. For example, a recession or industry-specific downturn can lead to reduced demand, lower sales, and decreased cash flow, making it challenging to service debt. Market and economic risks are often beyond the control of the company's management.
5. **Potential for Bankruptcy**: If the target company fails to generate sufficient cash flow, it may be unable to meet its debt obligations, leading to financial distress or bankruptcy. In such scenarios, lenders may seize the company's assets, and equity holders could lose their investment. The risk of insolvency is a critical consideration in LBO transactions.

Mitigating Risks in LBOs

1. **Thorough Due Diligence**: Conducting comprehensive due diligence is essential to understand the target company's financial health, operational capabilities, and market position.

This involves analyzing financial statements, assessing management quality, evaluating market conditions, and identifying potential risks. Thorough due diligence helps in making informed investment decisions and structuring the deal appropriately.
2. **Conservative Financing**: Avoiding excessive leverage by maintaining a balanced mix of debt and equity can reduce financial risk. Conservative financing ensures that the company has sufficient cash flow to service its debt and provides a buffer against unforeseen challenges. A prudent approach to financing enhances the company's financial stability and reduces the risk of default.
3. **Strategic Planning**: Developing robust post-acquisition plans to improve the target company's performance and manage debt effectively is crucial. This includes identifying operational inefficiencies, implementing cost-saving measures, and driving revenue growth. Strategic planning ensures that the company is well-positioned to achieve its financial targets and meet debt obligations.
4. **Contingency Planning**: Preparing for potential challenges by having contingency plans and reserve funds in place can mitigate risks. Contingency planning involves identifying potential risks, developing response strategies, and maintaining financial reserves to address unforeseen events. A proactive approach to risk management enhances the company's resilience and ability to navigate challenges.

Conclusion

Leveraged Buyouts (LBOs) offer a powerful mechanism for acquiring companies and achieving high returns on equity. However, they come with significant risks that require careful planning, thorough due diligence, and strategic management. By understanding the fundamentals of LBOs, their advantages, and associated risks, investors and acquiring companies can better navigate the complexities of these transactions and make informed decisions.

LBOs have been instrumental in the growth of private equity and have facilitated numerous high-profile acquisitions. The key to successful LBOs lies in selecting the right target, structuring the deal appropriately, securing favorable financing, and executing effective post-acquisition strategies. With careful planning and execution, LBOs can create substantial value for investors while driving growth and efficiency in the acquired companies.

Chapter 2: Mindset and Preparation
Developing the Right Mindset
Embracing the Entrepreneurial Spirit

Embarking on a journey of leveraged buyouts (LBOs) requires adopting an entrepreneurial mindset. This mindset is characterized by a willingness to take calculated risks, a proactive approach to problem-solving, and an unwavering commitment to innovation. Successful LBO practitioners are visionaries who can see potential where others see obstacles, and they possess the tenacity to drive improvements and efficiencies in their acquisitions.

1. **Stay Informed**: Continuous education is crucial. This means staying updated with the latest industry trends, market dynamics, and financial strategies. Read extensively—books, research papers, and articles on private equity, mergers and acquisitions (M&A), and corporate finance. Attend seminars, webinars, and conferences to learn from industry experts and network with peers. Following thought leaders on platforms like LinkedIn or subscribing to industry journals can also provide valuable insights.
2. **Be Resilient**: Resilience is a key trait in the entrepreneurial mindset. Setbacks and failures are inevitable in the world of LBOs. What distinguishes successful practitioners is their ability to learn from these experiences and persist despite obstacles. Cultivating resilience involves developing a positive outlook, maintaining flexibility in your strategies, and viewing challenges as opportunities for growth.
3. **Think Long-Term**: A long-term perspective is essential for LBO success. Rather than focusing on short-term gains, prioritize the sustainable growth and value creation of your acquisitions. This involves strategic planning, setting clear long-term goals, and aligning your efforts with these objectives. A long-term approach helps in building lasting value and ensuring the longevity and profitability of the acquired company.

Cultivating a Growth-Oriented Perspective

A growth-oriented perspective involves a relentless focus on continuous improvement, innovative thinking, and leadership development. This mindset is essential for driving the growth and success of acquired companies.

1. **Continuous Improvement**: Always look for ways to enhance operations, increase efficiency, and drive growth within the target company. This involves conducting regular performance reviews, benchmarking against industry standards, and implementing best practices. Encourage a culture of continuous improvement within the organization, where employees are motivated to identify and address inefficiencies.
2. **Innovative Thinking**: Innovation is a key driver of growth. Be open to new ideas and creative solutions that can enhance the value of the acquired company. This might involve adopting new technologies, exploring new market opportunities, or restructuring the business to improve efficiency. Encourage a culture of innovation where employees feel empowered to think creatively and propose new ideas.
3. **Leadership Development**: Strong leadership is crucial for driving change and achieving strategic goals. Invest in developing leadership within the acquired company. This involves identifying potential leaders, providing them with the necessary training and resources, and fostering a culture of leadership at all levels. Effective leaders can inspire teams, drive performance, and navigate the challenges of the LBO process.

Developing Financial Acumen

Understanding the financial aspects of LBOs is critical for success. This includes mastering financial statements, understanding leverage, and developing strong valuation skills.

1. **Mastering Financial Statements**: Being proficient in reading and interpreting financial statements is essential for assessing the financial health of potential acquisition targets. This includes understanding the income statement, balance sheet, and cash flow statement. Each of these financial statements provides critical insights into the company's performance, financial position, and cash flow generation capabilities.
2. **Understanding Leverage**: Leverage is the cornerstone of LBOs. It's crucial to understand how to use leverage effectively without overextending. This involves understanding the implications of different financing structures, interest rate environments, and debt covenants. Effective leverage management ensures that the company can meet its debt obligations and achieve the desired return on investment.
3. **Valuation Skills**: Accurate valuation of companies is a fundamental skill in LBOs. Develop the ability to value companies using various methods, such as discounted cash flow (DCF) analysis, EBITDA multiples, and comparable company analysis. Understanding these valuation techniques enables you to make informed decisions about potential acquisitions and negotiate favorable terms.

Understanding Risk and Reward
Identifying and Evaluating Risks

In LBOs, understanding and managing risks is crucial. The primary risks include financial, operational, and market risks.

1. **Financial Risk**: High leverage increases financial risk. Assess the target company's ability to generate sufficient cash flow to meet debt obligations. This involves analyzing historical cash flow generation, projecting future cash flows, and stress-testing these projections under different scenarios. A thorough understanding of the target company's financial risk profile helps in structuring the deal appropriately and mitigating potential risks.

2. **Operational Risk**: Evaluate the target company's operational efficiencies and potential areas for improvement. Identify any operational challenges that could impact performance, such as supply chain issues, production inefficiencies, or management weaknesses. Conducting a detailed operational due diligence helps in identifying these risks and developing strategies to address them.
3. **Market Risk**: Consider the broader market conditions and industry trends that could affect the target company's performance. This includes economic cycles, competitive dynamics, and regulatory changes. Conducting a thorough market analysis helps in understanding these risks and developing strategies to mitigate them.

Mitigating Risks

1. **Due Diligence**: Conduct thorough due diligence to uncover potential risks. This includes financial, legal, operational, and market due diligence. Thorough due diligence helps in identifying potential issues and developing strategies to address them.
2. **Diversification**: Diversify your investment portfolio to spread risk. Avoid putting all your resources into a single acquisition. Diversification helps in reducing the overall risk exposure and increasing the chances of success.
3. **Contingency Planning**: Develop contingency plans to address potential setbacks. This includes having financial reserves and alternative strategies in place. Contingency planning helps in ensuring that the company can navigate unforeseen challenges and continue to meet its strategic goals.

Balancing Risk and Reward

1. **Risk-Adjusted Returns**: Aim for investments that offer attractive risk-adjusted returns. This means evaluating the potential returns relative to the risks involved. Conduct a thorough risk-reward analysis to ensure that the potential rewards justify the risks.

2. **Strategic Synergies**: Look for acquisitions that offer strategic synergies, such as complementary products, expanded market reach, or enhanced operational efficiencies. These synergies can enhance the overall value of the acquisition and improve the risk-reward balance.

Assessing Personal and Financial Readiness
Personal Readiness

1. **Skills and Experience**: Assess whether you have the necessary skills and experience to execute an LBO successfully. This includes financial acumen, negotiation skills, and operational expertise. If you lack certain skills, consider partnering with experts or hiring advisors who can complement your strengths.
2. **Network and Resources**: Build a strong network of advisors, mentors, and industry contacts. Access to expert advice and resources can significantly enhance your chances of success. Networking helps in gaining valuable insights, identifying potential opportunities, and securing support during the LBO process.
3. **Commitment and Time**: Ensure you have the time and commitment required to manage an LBO. The process can be time-consuming and demanding, requiring focused attention and effort. Be prepared to dedicate significant time and resources to ensure the success of the acquisition.

Financial Readiness

1. **Capital Availability**: Evaluate your access to capital, including your own funds, investor commitments, and financing options. Ensure you have sufficient financial resources to support the acquisition and post-acquisition phases. Having access to adequate capital helps in securing the necessary financing and ensuring the smooth execution of the LBO.
2. **Risk Tolerance**: Assess your risk tolerance and financial stability. Be prepared for potential setbacks and ensure you have the financial resilience to weather challenges.

Understanding your risk tolerance helps in making informed decisions and managing potential risks effectively.
3. **Funding Strategies**: Develop a clear strategy for securing financing. This includes understanding the various financing options available, such as senior debt, mezzanine financing, and equity contributions. Having a well-defined funding strategy helps in securing the necessary financing and ensuring the success of the acquisition.

Building a Support Team

1. **Advisors and Mentors**: Assemble a team of experienced advisors and mentors who can provide guidance and support throughout the LBO process. This may include financial advisors, legal experts, and industry specialists. Having a strong support team helps in navigating the complexities of the LBO process and ensuring the success of the acquisition.
2. **Operational Team**: Identify key team members who will help manage the target company post-acquisition. This includes experienced managers, operational experts, and integration specialists. Having a strong operational team helps in ensuring the smooth transition and successful integration of the acquired company.
3. **Financial Partners**: Establish relationships with financial partners, such as banks, private equity firms, and institutional investors. Strong financial partnerships can provide the necessary support and resources for successful acquisitions. Having reliable financial partners helps in securing the necessary financing and ensuring the success of the acquisition.

Conclusion

Developing the right mindset and preparing thoroughly are critical steps in embarking on a leveraged buyout journey. By cultivating an entrepreneurial spirit, growth-oriented perspective, and financial acumen, you can position yourself for success. Understanding the intricacies of risk and reward and ensuring personal and financial readiness will further enhance your ability to navigate the complexities of LBOs effectively. Building a strong support team and leveraging expert advice will provide the necessary foundation for making informed decisions and achieving your strategic goals in the world of leveraged buyouts.

Chapter 3: Setting Acquisition Criteria
Identifying Target Industries
Industry Analysis and Selection

Selecting the right industry is a foundational step in the leveraged buyout (LBO) process. The industry you choose will significantly impact the acquisition's risk profile, growth potential, and overall success. A thorough industry analysis involves understanding market dynamics, growth prospects, the competitive landscape, and regulatory conditions.

1. **Market Dynamics**: Understanding the overall health and trends within the industry is crucial. Look for industries that are stable or growing rather than those in decline. Factors such as technological advancements, consumer behavior changes, and economic conditions play a pivotal role. For example, the technology sector has seen robust growth due to continuous innovation and increasing digital transformation across industries. In contrast, industries heavily reliant on outdated technologies may face decline.

    To analyze market dynamics, utilize tools like SWOT analysis (Strengths, Weaknesses, Opportunities, Threats) to evaluate the industry comprehensively. This analysis will help you identify the strengths and opportunities that can be leveraged and the weaknesses and threats that need to be mitigated.

2. **Growth Prospects**: Future growth potential is a key criterion. Industries poised for growth, driven by factors such as increasing demand, regulatory support, or emerging trends, are more attractive. For instance, the renewable energy sector is expected to grow significantly due to global shifts towards sustainable energy sources and supportive government policies.

    Evaluate growth prospects by examining industry reports, market research studies, and expert forecasts. Identify key drivers of growth, such as demographic shifts, technological advancements, or changes in consumer preferences. Understanding these drivers will help you predict the industry's future trajectory.

3. **Competitive Landscape**: Analyze the level of competition within the industry. Industries with high levels of competition might be challenging to enter and succeed in, whereas fragmented industries with numerous small players can offer consolidation opportunities. Assess the competitive dynamics by identifying key players, market share distribution, and competitive strategies.

   Porter's Five Forces analysis can be a useful tool for this purpose. It evaluates the competitive forces at play, including the threat of new entrants, bargaining power of suppliers and customers, threat of substitute products, and competitive rivalry. This analysis will help you understand the competitive intensity and identify potential competitive advantages.

4. **Regulatory Environment**: Regulatory stability and favorability are critical. Industries with stable regulatory environments are generally more attractive as they reduce the risk of unexpected changes that could impact operations. Conversely, industries subject to frequent regulatory changes or stringent regulations might pose additional risks.

   To assess the regulatory environment, review industry regulations, compliance requirements, and historical regulatory changes. Engage with legal experts and industry associations to gain insights into potential regulatory shifts and their implications. Understanding the regulatory landscape helps in identifying industries with a lower regulatory risk profile.

Key Factors for Industry Selection

1. **Profitability and Cash Flow**: Industries with a history of profitability and strong cash flow generation are ideal for LBOs. Stable and predictable cash flows are crucial for servicing the debt incurred during the buyout. Evaluate historical financial performance, profit margins, and cash flow stability within the industry.

   Analyze key financial ratios such as return on equity (ROE), return on assets (ROA), and operating margin to assess profitability. Additionally, review industry benchmarks and compare the target company's performance against these benchmarks. This analysis will help you identify industries with strong financial health and cash flow generation capabilities.

2. **Scalability**: Scalability potential is essential for LBO success. Industries that allow for significant growth without a proportionate increase in costs are more attractive. Scalability can be achieved through economies of scale, technological innovations, or market expansion.

   Evaluate scalability by assessing the industry's capacity for growth and identifying factors that facilitate scalability. For example, industries with high fixed costs and low variable costs often offer scalability potential, as additional revenue can be generated with minimal incremental costs. Understanding scalability helps in identifying industries where growth can be achieved efficiently.

3. **Barriers to Entry**: High barriers to entry can protect your acquisition from new competitors and secure its market position. These barriers could be in the form of capital requirements, intellectual property, regulatory approvals, or established brand reputation.

   Assess barriers to entry by identifying the factors that prevent new entrants from easily entering the industry. For example, industries with high capital requirements, complex regulatory approvals, or strong brand loyalty among customers often have high barriers to entry. Understanding these barriers helps in evaluating the competitive protection offered by the industry.

4. **Fragmentation and Consolidation Opportunities**: Fragmented industries present opportunities for consolidation, where you can acquire multiple smaller companies and combine them to achieve greater market power and operational efficiencies. Consolidation can lead to increased market share, improved bargaining power, and cost synergies.

    Evaluate industry fragmentation by analyzing the number and size distribution of companies within the industry. Identify opportunities for consolidation by assessing potential synergies, cost savings, and strategic benefits of combining multiple companies. Understanding industry fragmentation helps in identifying opportunities for value creation through consolidation.

Defining Company Size and Financial Metrics
Size Criteria

1. **Revenue and EBITDA**: Define the target company's size in terms of revenue and earnings before interest, taxes, depreciation, and amortization (EBITDA). Companies with stable and growing revenues, typically between £1 million and £100 million, are often ideal candidates for LBOs. EBITDA is a critical metric as it reflects the company's operating profitability and cash flow generation capability.

    Evaluate revenue and EBITDA trends over the past few years to assess stability and growth potential. Companies with consistent revenue growth and stable EBITDA margins are more attractive as they offer predictable cash flows and profitability. Additionally, compare the target company's financial performance against industry benchmarks to assess its relative position within the industry.

2. **Employee Count**: Consider the size of the workforce. Companies with a manageable number of employees are often easier to integrate and manage post-acquisition. However, the employee count should be sufficient to sustain operations and support growth initiatives.

Evaluate the employee count in relation to the company's revenue and operational complexity. Assess the organizational structure, key roles, and potential areas for improvement. Understanding the workforce size helps in identifying companies that can be effectively managed and scaled post-acquisition.

Financial Metrics

1. **Profit Margins**: Evaluate the target company's profit margins. Higher margins indicate a more efficient and profitable operation, which is desirable for LBOs. Gross margin, operating margin, and net margin are key indicators to consider.

Analyze historical profit margins and compare them to industry benchmarks. Companies with consistently high profit margins are more attractive as they offer better profitability and operational efficiency. Additionally, evaluate the factors driving profit margins, such as pricing power, cost structure, and operational efficiency. Understanding profit margins helps in assessing the company's financial health and profitability potential.

2. **Cash Flow Stability**: Ensure the target company has a history of stable and predictable cash flows. This is crucial for servicing the debt incurred during the buyout. Analyze historical cash flow statements and assess the consistency and predictability of cash flows.

Evaluate cash flow stability by analyzing cash flow trends, working capital management, and capital expenditure requirements. Companies with stable and predictable cash flows are more attractive as they offer better debt servicing capabilities and financial stability. Understanding cash flow stability helps in assessing the company's ability to generate consistent cash flows post-acquisition.

3. **Debt Levels**: Assess the target company's existing debt levels. Companies with low to moderate debt levels are more attractive as they offer greater flexibility for leveraging additional debt. High levels of existing debt can complicate the financing structure and increase financial risk.

    Evaluate the company's debt levels by analyzing the debt-to-equity ratio, interest coverage ratio, and debt servicing capabilities. Companies with manageable debt levels and strong debt servicing capabilities are more attractive as they offer better financial flexibility and lower financial risk. Understanding debt levels helps in assessing the company's financial stability and leveraging potential.

4. **Return on Investment (ROI)**: Estimate the potential ROI from the acquisition. This includes evaluating the expected internal rate of return (IRR) and the potential for value creation through operational improvements, cost synergies, and revenue growth.

    Calculate the potential ROI by analyzing the acquisition cost, projected cash flows, and exit strategy. Companies with high ROI potential and clear value creation opportunities are more attractive as they offer better returns and growth potential. Understanding ROI helps in assessing the financial attractiveness and value creation potential of the acquisition.

Geographic Considerations

Market Accessibility

1. **Local Market Presence**: Determine the target company's market presence and accessibility. Companies with a strong local market presence are often easier to manage and integrate. Additionally, understanding the local market dynamics can provide a strategic advantage.

   Evaluate the company's market presence by analyzing market share, customer base, and brand recognition within the local market. Companies with a strong local market presence and established customer relationships are more attractive as they offer better market penetration and customer loyalty. Understanding local market presence helps in assessing the company's competitive position and growth potential.

2. **Proximity to Key Markets**: Consider the target company's proximity to key markets. Being close to major markets can reduce transportation costs, improve supply chain efficiency, and enhance customer service. Proximity to suppliers and distribution channels is also a significant factor.

   Evaluate the company's geographic location by analyzing proximity to key markets, suppliers, and distribution channels. Companies located near key markets and suppliers are more attractive as they offer better operational efficiency and cost savings. Understanding proximity helps in assessing the company's logistical advantages and competitive position.

Economic and Political Stability

1. **Economic Conditions**: Evaluate the economic conditions of the target company's geographic location. Regions with stable and growing economies are more attractive as they offer a conducive environment for business growth and profitability.

Analyze economic indicators such as GDP growth, inflation rates, unemployment rates, and consumer spending trends. Regions with stable economic conditions and positive growth prospects are more attractive as they offer better market opportunities and financial stability. Understanding economic conditions helps in assessing the region's growth potential and business environment.

2. **Political Stability**: Assess the political stability of the region. Political instability can introduce significant risks, including regulatory changes, economic sanctions, and civil unrest. A stable political environment provides a predictable and secure operating environment.

    Evaluate political stability by analyzing historical political events, government policies, and geopolitical risks. Regions with stable political environments and supportive government policies are more attractive as they offer lower regulatory risks and operational disruptions. Understanding political stability helps in assessing the region's risk profile and business environment.

Regulatory Environment

1. **Local Regulations**: Understand the local regulatory environment. This includes tax policies, labor laws, environmental regulations, and industry-specific regulations. A favorable regulatory environment can reduce operational risks and compliance costs.

    Evaluate local regulations by reviewing tax policies, labor laws, environmental regulations, and compliance requirements. Regions with favorable regulatory environments and efficient legal processes are more attractive as they offer lower regulatory risks and compliance costs. Understanding local regulations helps in assessing the region's regulatory risk profile and business environment.

2. **Ease of Doing Business**: Consider the ease of doing business in the target company's location. This includes factors such as the efficiency of legal and bureaucratic processes, availability of skilled labor, and the overall business infrastructure. Regions with a high ease of doing business score are generally more attractive for acquisitions.

   Evaluate the ease of doing business by analyzing factors such as legal and bureaucratic efficiency, availability of skilled labor, infrastructure quality, and business environment. Regions with high ease of doing business scores offer better operational efficiency and lower operational risks. Understanding the ease of doing business helps in assessing the region's attractiveness and business environment.

Cultural and Language Considerations

1. **Cultural Compatibility**: Assess the cultural compatibility between your organization and the target company. Cultural differences can impact employee integration, management practices, and overall operational efficiency. Ensuring cultural alignment can facilitate a smoother integration process.

   Evaluate cultural compatibility by analyzing organizational culture, management practices, and employee values. Companies with compatible cultures and similar management practices are more attractive as they offer better integration and operational efficiency. Understanding cultural compatibility helps in assessing the company's integration potential and operational efficiency.

2. **Language Barriers**: Consider potential language barriers. Communication is critical during the acquisition and integration process. Ensuring that language differences do not hinder communication can prevent misunderstandings and operational disruptions.

Evaluate language barriers by analyzing the primary language of communication within the target company and the region. Companies with minimal language barriers are more attractive as they offer better communication and operational efficiency. Understanding language barriers helps in assessing the company's communication potential and operational efficiency.

Conclusion

Setting clear acquisition criteria is essential for identifying suitable LBO targets and ensuring the success of your acquisition strategy. By focusing on target industries, defining company size and financial metrics, and considering geographic factors, you can develop a robust framework for evaluating potential acquisition opportunities. This framework helps in identifying companies that not only fit your strategic objectives but also offer the potential for value creation and long-term success.

Chapter 4: Deal Sourcing Strategies
Leveraging Virtual Assistants
Role of Virtual Assistants in Deal Sourcing

Virtual assistants (VAs) play a crucial role in the deal sourcing process, offering valuable support to streamline and enhance your acquisition efforts. Their role extends beyond mere administrative tasks; they can be instrumental in conducting research, managing databases, and facilitating communication with potential targets. Here's a deeper dive into how VAs contribute to deal sourcing:

1. **Research and Data Gathering**: VAs can conduct comprehensive research on potential acquisition targets, scouring through various sources to gather essential data. This might include financial metrics, market trends, competitive analysis, and industry insights. By leveraging their research skills and access to online resources, VAs can provide you with valuable insights into potential targets, allowing you to make informed decisions.
2. **Database Management**: Maintaining an organized and up-to-date database of potential acquisition targets is essential for effective deal sourcing. VAs can help manage this database, ensuring that all relevant information is accurately recorded and easily accessible. They can update contact details, track communication history, and categorize targets based on specific criteria. This organized approach saves you time and effort when evaluating potential deals.
3. **Initial Outreach**: VAs can assist with the initial outreach to potential targets, helping you establish contact and initiate conversations. This might involve sending introductory emails, making follow-up calls, or scheduling meetings. VAs can handle the logistics of outreach, ensuring timely and professional communication with prospects. Their assistance in this stage of the process lays the foundation for building relationships with potential sellers and exploring acquisition opportunities.
4. **Administrative Tasks**: Beyond deal-specific activities, VAs can handle various administrative tasks to support your

overall acquisition efforts. This includes managing your calendar, organizing documents, preparing reports, and handling correspondence. By taking care of routine administrative duties, VAs free up your time to focus on high-level strategic activities, such as deal evaluation, negotiation, and execution.

Hiring and Managing Virtual Assistants

Hiring and managing virtual assistants effectively is crucial to maximizing their impact on your deal sourcing activities. Here are some best practices for hiring and managing VAs:

1. **Hiring Process**: When hiring a VA, clearly define the skills and qualifications you're looking for. Look for candidates with relevant experience in research, data management, communication, and organization. Platforms like Upwork, Fiverr, and Freelancer offer a pool of talented VAs with diverse skill sets. Take the time to review candidates' profiles, conduct interviews, and assess their suitability for the role.
2. **Training and Onboarding**: Provide comprehensive training to your VA to ensure they understand your business objectives, acquisition criteria, and specific tasks. This might include tutorials on using relevant tools and software, understanding your target market, and mastering communication protocols. Set clear expectations from the outset and provide ongoing support as needed.
3. **Tools and Technology**: Equip your VA with the necessary tools and technology to perform their tasks effectively. This might include access to project management software, CRM systems, communication platforms, and industry databases. Provide training on how to use these tools and ensure they have the technical support they need to troubleshoot any issues that arise.
4. **Performance Management**: Establish clear expectations and performance metrics for your VA. Regularly review their performance against these metrics and provide constructive feedback. Recognize their contributions and offer

opportunities for growth and development. Effective performance management ensures that your VA remains motivated, productive, and aligned with your acquisition goals.

Networking and Industry Connections
Building and Leveraging a Network

Networking is a powerful strategy for sourcing acquisition deals, providing access to exclusive opportunities and valuable insights. Building and leveraging a network requires proactive effort and strategic engagement. Here's how to effectively build and leverage your network for deal sourcing:

1. **Industry Conferences and Events**: Attend industry conferences, trade shows, and networking events to connect with potential sellers, industry experts, and other stakeholders. These events offer opportunities to build relationships, exchange ideas, and gain insights into market trends and potential acquisition targets. Be proactive in networking and engage with attendees to expand your professional circle.
2. **Professional Associations**: Join professional associations related to your target industry to access a network of like-minded professionals. These associations often host events, webinars, and networking opportunities that facilitate connections and knowledge sharing. Actively participate in association activities, contribute to discussions, and seek out opportunities to collaborate with fellow members.
3. **Online Networking**: Utilize online platforms such as LinkedIn to expand your professional network and connect with industry professionals, business owners, and potential sellers. Join relevant groups and communities, participate in discussions, and share valuable content to establish yourself as a thought leader in your field. Leverage LinkedIn's advanced search features to identify and reach out to potential contacts.

4. **Advisors and Intermediaries**: Build relationships with advisors, brokers, and intermediaries who specialize in your target industry. These professionals often have access to off-market deals and can provide valuable insights and introductions. Cultivate relationships with trusted advisors and leverage their expertise and networks to uncover hidden opportunities and navigate the acquisition process effectively.

Maintaining and Nurturing Relationships

Building a network is not just about making connections; it's about nurturing those relationships over time. Here are some strategies for maintaining and nurturing your network:

1. **Regular Communication**: Stay in touch with your network contacts through regular communication channels such as email, phone calls, and social media. Share relevant updates, industry news, and insights to keep them engaged and informed. Personalize your communication to show genuine interest and maintain rapport.
2. **Providing Value**: Focus on providing value to your network contacts by offering assistance, sharing resources, or making introductions. Look for opportunities to help others solve problems or achieve their goals. By providing value, you strengthen your relationships and build trust and goodwill within your network.
3. **Mutual Benefits**: Seek opportunities for mutual collaboration and benefit within your network. This might involve partnering on projects, exchanging referrals, or sharing industry expertise. Collaborative relationships foster mutual respect and reciprocity, leading to long-term partnerships and opportunities for growth.
4. **Networking Etiquette**: Follow networking etiquette to maintain professionalism and respect within your network. Be responsive to messages, show gratitude for assistance, and honor commitments. Respect others' time and boundaries, and avoid being overly aggressive or transactional in your

networking approach. Building authentic relationships based on mutual respect is key to long-term networking success.

Using Online Platforms and Resources
Online Deal Platforms

Online deal platforms offer a convenient and efficient way to source acquisition deals, providing access to a wide range of potential targets and valuable information. Here's how to effectively leverage online deal platforms:

1. **Defining Search Criteria**: Start by defining your search criteria based on your acquisition strategy and criteria. This might include industry, company size, financial metrics, geographic location, and other relevant factors. By narrowing down your search criteria, you can focus on opportunities that align with your objectives.
2. **Utilizing Filters and Alerts**: Most online platforms offer filters and alerts to help you find relevant listings. Take advantage of these features to customize your search and receive notifications of new opportunities that match your criteria. Set up alerts for specific keywords, industries, or geographic locations to stay informed about potential deals.
3. **Conducting Due Diligence**: Once you identify potential targets, conduct thorough due diligence to verify the information and assess the viability of the acquisition. This includes reviewing financial statements, conducting market analysis, and assessing operational capabilities. Use online resources and tools to gather relevant information and perform due diligence efficiently.
4. **Engaging with Sellers**: Reach out to potential sellers through the platform's communication tools. Craft personalized messages that demonstrate your interest in their business and highlight the value you can bring as a buyer. Be proactive in initiating conversations and follow up promptly to maintain momentum. Building rapport with sellers is essential for progressing the acquisition process and negotiating favorable terms.

Utilizing Online Resources

1. **Industry Databases and Directories**: Industry databases and directories are valuable resources for identifying potential acquisition targets and gathering essential information. These platforms provide detailed company profiles, contact details, financial metrics, and industry analysis. Examples include Hoover's, Dun & Bradstreet, and industry-specific directories. Utilize these resources to expand your target list and gain insights into market trends and competitors.
2. **Financial and Market Research Reports**: Access financial and market research reports to gain deeper insights into industry dynamics, competitive landscape, and potential acquisition opportunities. Platforms like IBISWorld, Statista, and MarketResearch.com offer comprehensive reports on various industries, including market size, growth trends, and key players. Analyze these reports to identify emerging trends, assess market opportunities, and validate your acquisition strategy.
3. **Company Websites and Social Media**: Conduct research on potential targets by visiting their company websites and social media profiles. Company websites provide valuable information about their products, services, customers, and achievements. Social media platforms such as LinkedIn, Twitter, and Facebook offer additional insights into their corporate culture, recent developments, and engagement with customers. Use these channels to gather intelligence, assess their online presence, and identify potential synergies.
4. **News and Industry Publications**: Stay updated on industry news and developments by subscribing to relevant publications and news outlets. Industry magazines, trade journals, and business news websites offer timely insights into market trends, regulatory changes, and company announcements. Monitor these sources regularly to stay informed about potential acquisition opportunities and emerging threats. Engage with industry publications to share your expertise, build your reputation, and expand your network.

Effective Use of Online Platforms

1. **Defining Search Criteria**: Clearly define your search criteria based on your acquisition strategy and objectives. This includes industry preferences, financial parameters, geographic preferences, and other relevant factors. By establishing clear criteria, you can focus your search efforts and identify opportunities that align with your investment thesis.
2. **Utilizing Filters and Alerts**: Take advantage of the filtering and alert features offered by online platforms to refine your search and stay informed about new listings. Customize your filters to match your specific criteria, such as revenue range, EBITDA multiple, or location. Set up alerts to receive notifications whenever new opportunities that meet your criteria are posted.
3. **Conducting Due Diligence**: Once you identify potential targets, conduct thorough due diligence to assess their financial health, operational performance, and growth prospects. Review financial statements, tax returns, customer contracts, and other relevant documents to validate their claims and identify potential risks. Utilize due diligence checklists and templates to ensure you cover all necessary areas and perform a comprehensive evaluation.
4. **Engaging with Sellers**: Engage with sellers proactively and professionally to express your interest in their business and initiate discussions. Craft tailored messages that demonstrate your understanding of their industry and articulate your value proposition as a buyer. Be prepared to answer questions and address concerns promptly to build trust and credibility. Maintain open communication channels throughout the negotiation process to facilitate a smooth transaction.

Conclusion

Effective deal sourcing requires a multifaceted approach that leverages virtual assistants, networking, and online platforms. Virtual assistants play a crucial role in conducting research, managing databases, and facilitating communication with potential targets. Networking provides access to exclusive opportunities and valuable insights, while online platforms offer a convenient way to identify and evaluate potential deals. By integrating these strategies and utilizing online resources effectively, you can expand your deal pipeline, uncover hidden opportunities, and ultimately find the right acquisition targets to support your growth objectives.

Chapter 5: Communicating with Sellers

In the process of pursuing leveraged buyouts (LBOs), effective communication with sellers is paramount. This chapter delves into the strategies and principles of communicating with sellers to establish rapport, build trust, and ultimately negotiate favorable deals.

Crafting Persuasive Letters and Emails

Effective communication through letters and emails is often the first step in initiating contact with potential sellers in the context of leveraged buyouts (LBOs). These initial communications serve as a crucial opportunity to introduce yourself, express interest in the seller's business, and lay the foundation for further discussions. Crafting persuasive letters and emails requires careful attention to detail, thoughtful messaging, and a clear understanding of the seller's perspective.

Personalization

Personalization is key to making your communication stand out and resonate with the recipient. Generic, templated messages are unlikely to capture the attention of potential sellers who receive numerous inquiries from interested buyers. Instead, take the time to research the company and its owners, understand their background and motivations, and tailor your communication accordingly. Address the seller by name, reference specific aspects of their business or industry, and demonstrate genuine interest in their success.

Clear Value Proposition

Your letter or email should clearly articulate the value proposition of your offer to the seller. This involves highlighting the benefits of selling their business to you, whether in terms of financial rewards, growth opportunities, or legacy preservation. Consider what sets your offer apart from others and why the seller should consider it. Focus on the unique strengths and advantages that you bring to the table as a buyer, whether it's your industry expertise, financial resources, or strategic vision.

Compelling Storytelling

Storytelling is a powerful technique for engaging the seller and conveying your vision for the future of their business. Instead of presenting dry facts and figures, use storytelling to paint a vivid picture of how their business could thrive under your ownership. Share success stories from your past acquisitions, highlight key milestones and achievements, and illustrate the potential for growth and innovation. By framing your offer within a compelling narrative, you can capture the seller's imagination and inspire confidence in your ability to realize their vision.

Professionalism and Respect

Maintaining a professional and respectful tone is essential when communicating with potential sellers. Avoid using overly aggressive or salesy language, as it can come across as off-putting or insincere. Instead, approach your communication with a mindset of mutual respect and understanding. Acknowledge the seller's accomplishments and contributions to their business, and demonstrate empathy for their concerns and objectives. Treat every interaction as an opportunity to build a positive relationship, regardless of the outcome of the negotiation.

Call to Action

Every letter or email should end with a clear call to action that prompts the seller to take the next step in the process. Whether it's scheduling a meeting, providing additional information, or starting a dialogue, make it easy for the seller to respond and engage with you further. Avoid leaving the conversation open-ended or ambiguous, as it can lead to confusion or inertia. By clearly outlining the next steps, you can keep the momentum going and move the negotiation forward.

Establishing Trust and Credibility

Building trust and credibility is essential for establishing a positive rapport with potential sellers and laying the groundwork for successful negotiations. In the context of leveraged buyouts, where sellers may have concerns about the future of their business post-acquisition, trust and credibility play an even more significant role. Here are strategies for establishing trust and credibility when communicating with sellers:

Active Listening

Active listening is a fundamental skill that involves fully engaging with the seller and demonstrating empathy and understanding. Take the time to listen to their concerns, objectives, and motivations, and show genuine interest in their perspective. Ask probing questions to uncover underlying issues or challenges, and validate their feelings and experiences. By listening attentively and empathetically, you can build trust and rapport with the seller and create a foundation for open and honest communication.

Transparency and Honesty

Transparency and honesty are essential pillars of trustworthiness. Be upfront and transparent about your intentions, capabilities, and limitations as a buyer. Avoid making exaggerated claims or misrepresentations, as they can undermine your credibility and erode trust. Instead, be honest about the risks and challenges involved in the acquisition process and discuss how you plan to address them. By demonstrating integrity and authenticity in your communication, you can build trust with the seller and establish yourself as a reliable and trustworthy partner.

Consistency and Reliability

Consistency and reliability are critical for building trust over time. Follow through on your commitments, meet deadlines, and maintain open lines of communication with the seller. Be proactive in providing updates and feedback, and ensure that you're accessible and responsive to their inquiries. By demonstrating consistency and reliability in your actions, you can reassure the seller that they can rely on you to deliver on your promises and commitments.

Professionalism and Integrity

Maintaining professionalism and integrity is essential throughout the negotiation process. Conduct yourself with honesty, integrity, and respect at all times, and adhere to ethical standards of conduct. Avoid engaging in deceptive or unethical practices, as they can damage your reputation and credibility. Instead, prioritize fairness, transparency, and mutual respect in your interactions with the seller. By upholding high standards of professionalism and integrity, you can earn the seller's trust and confidence and build a solid foundation for successful negotiations.

Building Mutual Respect

Building mutual respect is key to establishing a positive and productive relationship with the seller. Treat the seller with respect and dignity, regardless of the outcome of the negotiation. Acknowledge their expertise and accomplishments, and show appreciation for their contributions to their business. Foster a collaborative and cooperative atmosphere where both parties feel valued and respected. By building mutual respect, you can create a conducive environment for open communication, constructive dialogue, and successful negotiations.

Emphasizing Safety and Stability

In the context of leveraged buyouts, where sellers may have concerns about the future of their business post-acquisition, emphasizing safety and stability is essential. Sellers want assurance that their business will be in safe hands and that the transition will be smooth and seamless. Here's how to address seller concerns and risks and emphasize safety and stability:

Financial Strength and Resources

Highlight your financial strength and resources as a buyer to reassure the seller that you have the capability to complete the transaction and support the ongoing operations of the business. Provide evidence of your financial stability, such as audited financial statements, bank statements, or letters of credit. Assure the seller that you have the necessary resources to invest in the business and drive growth and innovation.

Track Record and Experience

Showcase your track record and experience in acquiring and managing businesses to demonstrate your competence and credibility as a buyer. Provide examples of successful acquisitions and value creation initiatives that you've undertaken in the past. Highlight your industry expertise, operational capabilities, and strategic vision for the future of the business. By demonstrating your proven track record and experience, you can instill confidence in the seller and alleviate concerns about the transition process.

Long-Term Vision and Commitment

Communicate your long-term vision for the acquired business and your commitment to its success and sustainability. Assure the seller that you're not merely looking for a short-term gain, but rather, are invested in the long-term growth and prosperity of the business. Discuss your strategic plans for the business, including expansion opportunities, product development initiatives, and talent acquisition strategies. By emphasizing your long-term vision and commitment, you can reassure the seller that their business will be in good hands under your ownership.

Risk Mitigation Strategies

Address potential risks and challenges proactively and discuss your risk mitigation strategies and contingency plans. Identify key risks associated with the acquisition, such as market volatility, regulatory changes, or operational disruptions, and outline how you intend to mitigate them. Discuss your plans for preserving the business's core operations, retaining key employees, and maintaining customer relationships during the transition period. Highlight your ability to adapt to changing market conditions and navigate unforeseen challenges effectively. By demonstrating your proactive approach to risk management, you can reassure the seller that their business will be well-protected under your ownership.

Collaborative Approach

Adopt a collaborative approach to negotiation and decision-making to foster trust and cooperation with the seller. Involve the seller in discussions about the future direction of the business and seek their input and feedback on key decisions. Create opportunities for open dialogue and constructive exchange of ideas, and be receptive to the seller's concerns and suggestions. By involving the seller in the decision-making process and treating them as a valued partner, you can build a strong foundation for a successful and mutually beneficial relationship.

Communication of Stability Measures

Clearly communicate the stability measures you plan to implement to ensure a smooth transition and minimize disruptions to the business operations. This may include retaining key employees, honoring existing contracts and agreements, and maintaining continuity in customer relationships. Assure the seller that you have a detailed transition plan in place, outlining the steps you'll take to preserve the business's stability and capitalize on growth opportunities. By demonstrating your commitment to maintaining stability and continuity, you can alleviate the seller's concerns and instill confidence in the future of their business under your ownership.

Assurance of Legacy Preservation

Acknowledge the seller's legacy and the significance of their contribution to the business. Assure them that you respect their legacy and are committed to preserving it under your ownership.

Discuss how you plan to build upon the seller's achievements and honor their legacy through continued success and growth. By showing appreciation for the seller's legacy and commitment to preserving it, you can build trust and goodwill and create a positive foundation for the negotiation process.

Conclusion

Effective communication with sellers is essential for establishing trust, building rapport, and ultimately negotiating successful deals in the context of leveraged buyouts. By emphasizing safety and stability, and demonstrating transparency, integrity, and collaboration, you can alleviate the seller's concerns and instill confidence in the future of their business under your ownership. By fostering a positive and constructive relationship with the seller, you can pave the way for a smooth and successful transition and set the stage for long-term success and growth.

Chapter 6: Best Sectors to Target

Choosing the right sector to target is a crucial decision in the process of pursuing leveraged buyouts (LBOs). Different industries present varying levels of opportunity, growth potential, and stability, which can significantly impact the success of your acquisition strategy. This chapter explores the key considerations for identifying the best sectors to target in LBOs.

Analyzing Industry Trends and Opportunities

Analyzing industry trends and opportunities is a fundamental step in identifying the best sectors to target for leveraged buyouts (LBOs). This process involves conducting thorough market research and analysis to understand the dynamics shaping different industries and to uncover investment opportunities.

Market Research and Analysis

Market research forms the foundation of analyzing industry trends and opportunities. This involves gathering and analyzing data on market size, growth rates, consumer behavior, competitive landscape, and regulatory environment within various sectors. Utilizing industry reports, market studies, economic forecasts, and government data sources can provide valuable insights into the current state and future outlook of different industries.

For example, suppose you're considering investing in the renewable energy sector. In that case, you might analyze market reports detailing the growth of renewable energy sources, government incentives for clean energy adoption, technological advancements in solar and wind energy, and the impact of regulatory policies on the industry.

Technological Advancements and Innovation

Technological advancements and innovation play a significant role in shaping industry trends and opportunities. Industries that are at the forefront of technological innovation often present attractive investment opportunities due to their potential for rapid growth and disruption of traditional business models.

For instance, sectors such as artificial intelligence, biotechnology, renewable energy, and e-commerce have seen significant technological advancements in recent years, creating opportunities for investors to capitalize on emerging trends and disruptive technologies.

Regulatory Environment

The regulatory environment is another critical factor to consider when analyzing industry trends and opportunities. Regulatory policies and government interventions can have a profound impact on different sectors, influencing market dynamics, investment opportunities, and growth prospects.

For example, industries such as healthcare, financial services, and energy are subject to extensive regulatory oversight, with changes in regulations often shaping market trends and investment opportunities. Understanding the regulatory landscape within each sector is essential for assessing potential risks and opportunities and making informed investment decisions.

Evaluating Growth Potential and Stability

Assessing the growth potential and stability of different sectors is essential for identifying attractive investment opportunities and mitigating risks associated with leveraged buyouts. This involves evaluating various factors, including market dynamics, demand drivers, industry lifecycle stage, and competitive landscape.

Market Dynamics and Demand Drivers

Understanding the underlying market dynamics and demand drivers within different sectors is critical for assessing their growth potential and stability. Industries with strong demand drivers such as demographic trends, consumer preferences, and macroeconomic factors are more likely to experience consistent growth and stability over the long term.

For example, sectors such as healthcare, technology, and consumer goods often benefit from demographic trends such as population growth, aging populations, and changing consumer preferences, driving sustained demand for products and services.

Industry Lifecycle Stage

Assessing the stage of the industry lifecycle is another important consideration when evaluating growth potential and stability. Industries go through different stages of development, including introduction, growth, maturity, and decline, each presenting unique opportunities and challenges for investors.

For instance, industries in the early stages of development or experiencing rapid growth may offer attractive investment prospects due to their potential for high returns and market expansion. Conversely, mature industries may offer more stable but slower-growing investment opportunities.

Competitive Landscape

Evaluating the competitive landscape within different sectors is essential for assessing growth potential and stability. Industries with fragmented competition or low barriers to entry may present opportunities for consolidation and market leadership, while industries with high barriers to entry or intense competition may pose challenges for investors.

For example, industries such as technology, healthcare, and telecommunications often feature high levels of competition and rapid innovation, creating opportunities for companies to differentiate themselves and capture market share. Understanding the competitive dynamics within each sector is crucial for identifying opportunities for value creation and growth.

Assessing Competitive Landscape

Assessing the competitive landscape within different sectors is essential for identifying attractive investment opportunities and understanding the dynamics shaping industry trends and opportunities. This involves evaluating factors such as industry concentration, competitive advantage, and innovation to assess the level of competition and market dynamics within each sector.

Industry Concentration and Market Share

Industry concentration and market share distribution are important indicators of the competitive landscape within different sectors. Industries with a few dominant players or a high degree of consolidation may present challenges for new entrants seeking to gain market share, while industries with a more fragmented competitive landscape may offer opportunities for market expansion and growth.

For example, industries such as technology, healthcare, and financial services often feature high levels of consolidation, with a few dominant players controlling significant market share. Understanding the level of industry concentration and market share distribution is essential for assessing competitive dynamics and identifying opportunities for market entry and growth.

Competitive Advantage and Differentiation

Assessing competitive advantage and differentiation is critical for understanding the competitive landscape within different sectors. Industries where companies have established strong brand equity, proprietary technology, or economies of scale may present attractive investment opportunities due to their ability to outperform competitors and generate superior returns.

For example, companies such as Apple, Google, and Amazon have built sustainable competitive advantages through innovation, brand loyalty, and customer experience, allowing them to maintain market leadership and drive long-term growth. Identifying sectors where companies have established competitive advantages is essential for identifying opportunities for value creation and growth.

Innovation and Disruption

Innovation and disruption play a significant role in shaping the competitive landscape within different sectors. Industries that are undergoing rapid technological change and disruption may present opportunities for new entrants to disrupt incumbents and gain market share, while also presenting challenges for existing players to adapt and maintain their competitive position.

Industry Trends and Emerging Technologies

Analyzing industry trends and emerging technologies is essential for identifying opportunities for innovation and disruption within different sectors. Industries that are embracing new technologies and business models may present attractive investment opportunities due to their potential for rapid growth and market expansion.

For example, sectors such as artificial intelligence, blockchain, and renewable energy are experiencing significant innovation and disruption, creating opportunities for investors to capitalize on emerging trends and technologies. Understanding industry trends and the adoption of new technologies is crucial for identifying opportunities for value creation and growth.

Competitive Dynamics and Market Positioning

Assessing competitive dynamics and market positioning is essential for understanding the competitive landscape within different sectors. Industries with intense competition and low barriers to entry may present challenges for investors seeking to establish a competitive advantage, while industries with high barriers to entry or differentiated business models may offer opportunities for market leadership and growth.

For example, industries such as telecommunications, automotive, and retail often feature intense competition and price competition, making it challenging for companies to differentiate themselves and capture market share. Understanding competitive dynamics and market positioning is crucial for identifying opportunities for strategic differentiation and value creation.

Regulatory Environment and Compliance

Evaluating the regulatory environment and compliance requirements within different sectors is essential for assessing competitive dynamics and market opportunities. Industries that are subject to extensive regulatory oversight or facing regulatory uncertainty may pose challenges for investors, while industries with favorable regulatory trends or undergoing deregulation may present opportunities for market expansion and growth.

For example, industries such as healthcare, financial services, and energy are subject to complex regulatory frameworks, with changes in regulations often shaping market dynamics and investment opportunities. Understanding the regulatory environment and compliance requirements within each sector is essential for identifying opportunities for value creation and growth.

Conclusion

Analyzing the competitive landscape within different sectors is essential for identifying attractive investment opportunities and understanding the dynamics shaping industry trends and opportunities. By assessing factors such as industry concentration, competitive advantage, innovation, and regulatory environment, investors can identify sectors that offer the greatest potential for value creation and growth. By staying informed about industry trends and emerging technologies, investors can position themselves to capitalize on opportunities for innovation and disruption and drive long-term success in the leveraged buyout process.

Chapter 7: Understanding Valuation Methods

Valuation is a critical aspect of the leveraged buyout (LBO) process, as it determines the price that the buyer is willing to pay for the target company. Various valuation methods can be employed to assess the fair value of a business and inform the decision-making process. This chapter explores three commonly used valuation methods in LBOs: Discounted Cash Flow (DCF) analysis, Earnings Before Interest, Taxes, Depreciation, and Amortization (EBITDA) and Free Cash Flow (FCF) multiples, and comparables and market analysis.

Discounted Cash Flow (DCF) Analysis

Discounted Cash Flow (DCF) analysis is a fundamental valuation method used in leveraged buyouts (LBOs) to estimate the intrinsic value of a business based on its future cash flow projections. This method relies on the principle that the value of a business is determined by the present value of its expected future cash flows.

Forecasting Future Cash Flows

Forecasting future cash flows is a critical aspect of DCF analysis. This involves projecting the cash flows that the target company is expected to generate over a specified period, typically ranging from five to ten years. Cash flows are typically estimated on an annual basis and include operating cash flows, capital expenditures, working capital changes, and taxes.

To forecast future cash flows accurately, analysts must consider various factors such as industry trends, market dynamics, competitive landscape, and macroeconomic conditions. They may utilize historical financial data, industry research, management forecasts, and market intelligence to inform their projections.

Determining Discount Rate

The discount rate used in DCF analysis represents the rate of return that investors require to compensate them for the time value of money and the risk associated with investing in the target company. The most commonly used discount rate is the weighted average cost of capital (WACC), which reflects the weighted average of the cost of equity and the cost of debt.

The cost of equity is determined using the capital asset pricing model (CAPM) or other equity risk premium models, taking into account factors such as the risk-free rate, market risk premium, and beta coefficient. The cost of debt is calculated based on the company's borrowing costs, taking into consideration factors such as interest rates, credit spreads, and debt maturity.

Calculating Terminal Value

In DCF analysis, the terminal value represents the value of the business at the end of the forecast period and accounts for all future cash flows beyond the explicit forecast period. Terminal value can be estimated using the perpetuity growth method or the exit multiple method.

The perpetuity growth method assumes that the business will continue to generate cash flows at a constant growth rate indefinitely beyond the forecast period. The exit multiple method, on the other hand, applies a valuation multiple, such as the price-to-earnings (P/E) ratio or the enterprise value-to-EBITDA ratio, to a measure of future cash flows or earnings to estimate the terminal value.

Summing Present Values

Once the future cash flows and terminal value have been estimated, they are discounted back to their present value using the discount rate. The present value of each cash flow is calculated by dividing it by the discount rate raised to the power of the corresponding time period. The present values of all cash flows are then summed to derive the total enterprise value of the business.

EBITDA and Free Cash Flow (FCF) Multiples

EBITDA and Free Cash Flow (FCF) multiples are commonly used in LBOs to assess the relative valuation of a target company compared to its peers. These multiples provide a quick and straightforward method for estimating the value of a business based on its earnings or cash flow metrics.

Selecting Comparable Companies

The first step in using EBITDA and FCF multiples for valuation is to identify a group of comparable companies within the same industry or sector. These comparable companies should have similar business models, revenue streams, growth prospects, and risk profiles as the target company.

Analysts typically select comparable companies based on factors such as industry classification, market capitalization, geographic location, and business segment. They may utilize financial databases, industry reports, and market intelligence to identify appropriate comparables for valuation purposes.

Calculating Multiples

Once the comparable companies have been identified, analysts calculate EBITDA and FCF multiples for each company by dividing its enterprise value (EV) or equity value (EV) by its EBITDA or FCF, respectively. Enterprise value represents the total value of a company's equity and debt, while equity value represents the value of its equity shareholders.

EBITDA and FCF multiples provide a simple yet effective way to assess the relative valuation of the target company compared to its peers. By comparing the target company's multiples to those of the comparable companies, analysts can gauge its valuation relative to the market and identify potential valuation discrepancies.

Applying Multiples to Target Company

Once the multiples have been calculated for the comparable companies, analysts apply the average or median multiples to the target company's EBITDA or FCF to estimate its implied enterprise value or equity value. This approach allows analysts to assess the target company's valuation based on market-based metrics and benchmark it against its peers.

Adjusting for Differences

It's important to note that not all companies are directly comparable, and adjustments may be necessary to account for differences in growth rates, risk profiles, and other relevant factors between the target company and the comparable companies. Analysts may apply adjustments such as growth rate differentials, risk premium adjustments, and size adjustments to align the target company's valuation with its peers.

Comparables and Market Analysis

Comparables and market analysis involve comparing the financial performance and valuation metrics of the target company to those of similar companies in the market. This method provides valuable insights into the relative valuation of the target company within its industry or sector and helps identify potential valuation discrepancies.

Identifying Comparable Companies

The first step in conducting comparables and market analysis is to identify a group of comparable companies that operate in the same industry or sector as the target company. These comparable companies should have similar business models, revenue streams, growth prospects, and risk profiles as the target company.

Analysts typically select comparable companies based on factors such as industry classification, market capitalization, geographic location, and business segment. They may utilize financial databases, industry reports, and market intelligence to identify appropriate comparables for analysis.

Analyzing Financial Performance

Once the comparable companies have been identified, analysts analyze their financial performance to assess their relative strength and competitive position. This includes evaluating key financial metrics such as revenue growth, profitability, margins, return on investment, and market share.

Comparing the target company's financial performance to that of its peers allows analysts to identify areas of strength and weakness and assess its competitive position within the market. This analysis provides valuable insights into the target company's relative valuation and helps identify potential opportunities for value creation.

Comparing Valuation Metrics

In addition to analyzing financial performance, analysts compare the valuation metrics of the target company to those of its peers to assess its relative valuation. This includes comparing metrics such as the price-to-earnings (P/E) ratio, price-to-sales (P/S) ratio, price-to-book (P/B) ratio, and EV/EBITDA ratio.

By benchmarking the target company's valuation metrics against those of its peers, analysts can identify potential valuation discrepancies and assess its relative valuation within the market. This analysis provides valuable insights into the target company's valuation relative to its peers and helps inform investment decisions.

Assessing Market Trends

Finally, analysts assess market trends and industry dynamics to gauge the potential impact on the target company's future performance and valuation. This includes analyzing factors such as changes in consumer behavior, technological advancements, regulatory developments, and competitive pressures.

Understanding market trends and industry dynamics allows analysts to assess the target company's growth prospects, competitive position, and valuation relative to the market. This analysis provides valuable context for interpreting financial performance and valuation metrics and helps inform investment decisions.

Conclusion

Understanding valuation methods is essential for effectively evaluating investment opportunities in leveraged buyouts (LBOs). Discounted Cash Flow (DCF analysis, EBITDA and Free Cash Flow (FCF) multiples, and comparables and market analysis are three commonly used methods for assessing the value of a target company in an LBO. Each method offers unique insights into the intrinsic value of the business and helps investors make informed decisions about potential acquisitions.

Integrating Valuation Methods

While each valuation method has its strengths and limitations, integrating multiple methods can provide a more comprehensive assessment of the target company's value. By using a combination of DCF analysis, multiples analysis, and market analysis, investors can triangulate their valuation estimates and gain a more robust understanding of the target company's value.

For example, DCF analysis provides a detailed assessment of the target company's future cash flow potential, taking into account factors such as growth rates, profitability, and risk. Multiples analysis, on the other hand, offers a quick and straightforward way to assess the target company's valuation relative to its peers in the market. Market analysis provides context for interpreting financial performance and valuation metrics by analyzing industry trends, competitive dynamics, and market positioning.

Considering Limitations and Assumptions

It's important to recognize that all valuation methods are based on certain assumptions and have inherent limitations. For example,

DCF analysis relies on forecasts of future cash flows, which are subject to uncertainty and may be influenced by factors such as changes in market conditions, competitive pressures, and regulatory developments. Multiples analysis relies on the selection of comparable companies, which may not always be directly comparable to the target company in terms of size, growth, or risk profile.

Investors should carefully consider the assumptions underlying each valuation method and critically evaluate the reliability of their estimates. Sensitivity analysis can be used to assess the impact of changes in key assumptions on the target company's valuation and to quantify the level of uncertainty associated with the valuation estimates.

Leveraging Professional Expertise

Valuation is both an art and a science, requiring a blend of quantitative analysis, industry expertise, and judgment. While investors can perform their own valuations using publicly available data and financial models, they may also benefit from leveraging professional expertise, such as investment bankers, financial advisors, and valuation experts.

Professional advisors can provide valuable insights into industry trends, market dynamics, and valuation methodologies, helping investors make more informed decisions about potential acquisitions. They can also assist with conducting due diligence, negotiating deal terms, and structuring the transaction to maximize value and mitigate risks.

Conclusion

Valuation is a critical aspect of the leveraged buyout (LBO) process, as it determines the price that the buyer is willing to pay for the target company. Discounted Cash Flow (DCF) analysis, EBITDA and Free Cash Flow (FCF) multiples, and comparables and market analysis are three commonly used methods for assessing the value of a target company in an LBO. Each method offers unique insights into the intrinsic value of the business and helps investors make informed decisions about potential acquisitions.

By integrating multiple valuation methods, considering limitations and assumptions, and leveraging professional expertise, investors can perform robust valuations and make well-informed investment decisions in the context of leveraged buyouts. Valuation is a dynamic process that requires careful analysis, judgment, and consideration of all relevant factors to arrive at a fair and reasonable price for the target company.

Chapter 8: Negotiating the Deal

Negotiating the deal is a crucial phase in the leveraged buyout (LBO) process, where both the buyer and the seller aim to reach a mutually beneficial agreement. This chapter explores various strategies for negotiating the deal, including achieving win-win outcomes, balancing price, terms, and conditions, and effectively handling counteroffers and objections.

Strategies for Win-Win Negotiations

Negotiating a leveraged buyout (LBO) deal is not just about securing the best terms for the buyer; it's about reaching an agreement that satisfies both parties and sets the stage for a successful transaction and post-acquisition relationship. Win-win negotiations involve strategies that prioritize mutual benefit and collaboration.

Establishing Trust and Rapport

Building trust and rapport with the seller is essential for fostering a positive negotiation environment. Trust is the foundation of any successful negotiation, as it enables open communication, promotes transparency, and facilitates cooperation between parties. Establishing trust begins with demonstrating honesty, integrity, and reliability in all interactions with the seller. Building rapport involves finding common ground, showing genuine interest in the seller's perspective, and fostering a sense of camaraderie and goodwill.

Identifying Shared Goals and Interests

Identifying shared goals and interests between the buyer and the seller is key to aligning their objectives and facilitating win-win negotiations. While both parties may have different motivations for the deal, there are often underlying objectives that they both value. For example, both parties may be interested in maximizing the value of the transaction, minimizing risk, and ensuring a smooth transition. By focusing on these shared goals and interests, negotiations can be framed in a way that emphasizes collaboration and mutual benefit.

Creating Value for Both Parties

Seeking opportunities to create value for both parties can enhance the likelihood of reaching a successful agreement. Creating value involves finding ways to maximize the benefits of the transaction for both the buyer and the seller. This may include exploring creative deal structures, offering incentives or concessions, or finding solutions that address the seller's non-financial objectives, such as preserving their legacy or ensuring the well-being of employees. By demonstrating a willingness to create value for the seller, the buyer can build goodwill and strengthen the negotiation position.

Maintaining Flexibility and Adaptability

Remaining flexible and adaptable throughout the negotiation process is essential for navigating unexpected challenges and finding mutually acceptable solutions. Negotiations rarely proceed exactly as planned, and both parties may need to make concessions or adjust their positions to reach an agreement. By remaining open to new ideas, being willing to compromise on certain terms, and exploring alternative options, both parties can work together to overcome obstacles and find common ground.

Balancing Price, Terms, and Conditions

Negotiating the price, terms, and conditions of an LBO deal requires careful consideration of various factors and trade-offs. Balancing these elements effectively is essential for reaching a mutually beneficial agreement that satisfies both the buyer and the seller.

Evaluating Trade-offs

Balancing price, terms, and conditions involves evaluating trade-offs between different aspects of the deal. For example, increasing the purchase price may require accepting less favorable terms or conditions, while negotiating more favorable terms may involve adjusting the purchase price accordingly. Understanding the interplay between price, terms, and conditions is crucial for making informed negotiation decisions and maximizing value for both parties.

Prioritizing Key Objectives

Identifying and prioritizing key objectives is essential for focusing negotiations on the most critical aspects of the deal. Prioritization helps both parties clarify their goals and understand the relative importance of different terms and conditions. By prioritizing key objectives upfront, negotiations can be streamlined, and potential areas of contention can be addressed more efficiently.

Seeking Creative Solutions

Seeking creative solutions to address conflicting interests and overcome obstacles can help bridge the gap between buyer and seller expectations. Creative solutions may involve exploring alternative financing structures, adjusting payment terms, or incorporating earn-outs or performance-based incentives into the deal. By thinking outside the box and being open to new ideas, both parties can find innovative ways to structure the deal that maximize value and mitigate risk.

Anticipating Future Implications

Considering the long-term implications of different price, terms, and conditions is essential for making informed negotiation decisions. Anticipating how certain terms may impact post-acquisition integration, ongoing operations, and future growth can help both parties assess the value and risk associated with the deal. By taking a forward-thinking approach to negotiation, both parties can ensure that the terms of the deal align with their long-term strategic objectives and maximize value over time.

Handling Counteroffers and Objections

Effectively handling counteroffers and objections is a critical aspect of negotiating an LBO deal. Counteroffers and objections are inevitable in any negotiation, and how they are addressed can significantly impact the outcome of the deal.

Active Listening and Understanding

Active listening and understanding are essential for effectively addressing counteroffers and objections. Instead of dismissing the seller's concerns or objections, the buyer should take the time to listen attentively, ask clarifying questions, and seek to understand the underlying reasons behind the objections. By demonstrating empathy and showing a genuine interest in addressing the seller's concerns, the buyer can build trust and credibility and facilitate more productive negotiations.

Providing Clear and Transparent Communication

Providing clear and transparent communication throughout the negotiation process is crucial for building trust and maintaining goodwill with the seller. The buyer should clearly articulate the rationale behind their proposals, explain the benefits of the deal, and address any concerns or objections in a timely and transparent manner. By providing clear and honest communication, the buyer can alleviate seller apprehensions and facilitate progress towards a final agreement.

Offering Compromises and Solutions

Offering compromises and solutions to address seller objections can help move negotiations forward and reach a resolution. Instead of simply rejecting the seller's objections or insisting on their own terms, the buyer should seek to find common ground and explore alternative solutions that meet the needs of both parties. This may involve revisiting certain terms or conditions, providing additional assurances or protections, or offering incentives to sweeten the deal for the seller.

Maintaining Professionalism and Respect

Maintaining professionalism and respect during negotiations is essential for preserving positive relationships and fostering a collaborative negotiation environment. The buyer should avoid confrontational or adversarial tactics, remain patient and composed, and treat the seller with courtesy and respect at all times. By demonstrating professionalism and respect, the buyer can build trust and goodwill with the seller and increase the likelihood of reaching a mutually acceptable agreement.

Conclusion

Negotiating the deal in an LBO requires a strategic and collaborative approach that prioritizes mutual benefit and cooperation. By employing strategies for win-win negotiations, balancing price, terms, and conditions, and effectively handling counteroffers and objections, both parties can work towards reaching a mutually beneficial agreement that sets the stage for a successful transaction and post-acquisition relationship.

Negotiating an LBO deal is a complex and multifaceted process that requires careful consideration of various factors and trade-offs. By employing strategies for win-win negotiations, both the buyer and the seller can work together to create value, build trust, and reach a mutually acceptable agreement. Balancing price, terms, and conditions involves evaluating trade-offs, prioritizing key objectives, seeking creative solutions, and anticipating future implications. Handling counteroffers and objections requires active listening, clear communication, offering compromises, and maintaining professionalism and respect.

Successful negotiation in an LBO requires patience, flexibility, and a commitment to finding common ground. By approaching negotiations with a collaborative mindset and a focus on mutual benefit, both parties can navigate the complexities of the deal-making process and achieve their respective objectives.

In conclusion, negotiating the deal in an LBO is a critical step in the transaction process that requires careful planning, effective communication, and strategic decision-making. By employing the strategies outlined in this chapter, both the buyer and the seller can work towards reaching a mutually beneficial agreement that maximizes value and sets the stage for a successful partnership.

Chapter 9: Deal Structure and Financing

The structure of a leveraged buyout (LBO) deal plays a crucial role in determining its success and the ability of the buyer to finance the acquisition. This chapter explores various deal structures and financing options available to buyers, including asset-based lending, invoice financing, merchant financing, and leveraging target company assets and cash reserves.

Exploring Different Financing Options
Asset-Based Lending (ABL)

Asset-based lending (ABL) is a flexible financing option that provides borrowers with access to capital by leveraging their assets as collateral. In an ABL arrangement, the lender advances funds based on the value of the borrower's assets, such as accounts receivable, inventory, equipment, or real estate. These assets serve as security for the loan, providing the lender with a form of recourse in the event of default.

One of the key advantages of ABL is its flexibility compared to traditional forms of financing. Since the loan is secured by tangible assets, ABL lenders are typically more willing to extend credit to borrowers with less-than-perfect credit histories or limited operating histories. Additionally, ABL facilities can be structured to provide ongoing working capital, enabling borrowers to access funds as needed to support day-to-day operations or finance growth initiatives.

ABL arrangements typically involve a borrowing base calculation, which determines the maximum amount that the borrower can borrow based on the value of eligible collateral. The borrowing base may be subject to periodic adjustments to reflect changes in the value of the collateral or the borrower's financial condition. As a result, ABL facilities provide borrowers with a flexible source of financing that can adapt to their changing needs over time.

Invoice Financing

Invoice financing, also known as accounts receivable financing or factoring, is a financing option that allows businesses to convert outstanding invoices into immediate cash. In an invoice financing arrangement, the borrower sells its accounts receivable to a third-party lender, known as the factor, at a discount. The factor advances a percentage of the face value of the invoices to the borrower upfront, typically ranging from 70% to 90%, with the remainder held in reserve.

Invoice financing provides businesses with access to working capital by accelerating the collection of accounts receivable, improving cash flow, and reducing the need for short-term borrowing. This type of financing is particularly well-suited for businesses with long payment cycles or seasonal fluctuations in cash flow, as it provides them with a steady source of liquidity to support ongoing operations.

One of the key advantages of invoice financing is its speed and simplicity compared to traditional forms of financing. Since the loan is secured by the accounts receivable, rather than the borrower's creditworthiness, approval and funding can be completed quickly, often within a matter of days. Additionally, invoice financing does not require businesses to take on additional debt or dilute equity, making it an attractive option for businesses looking to preserve financial flexibility.

Merchant Financing

Merchant financing, also known as revenue-based financing or merchant cash advances, is a financing option that provides businesses with upfront capital in exchange for a percentage of future sales or revenue. In a merchant financing arrangement, the lender advances funds to the borrower based on its projected future revenue, typically ranging from 10% to 30% of monthly revenue. The borrower repays the advance, plus a fee or percentage, by remitting a fixed percentage of its daily or weekly sales to the lender until the advance is repaid in full.

Merchant financing offers businesses a flexible and accessible source of capital to support growth initiatives, finance working capital needs, or fund acquisitions. Unlike traditional loans, merchant financing does not require businesses to make fixed monthly payments or adhere to a predetermined repayment schedule. Instead, repayment is tied to the borrower's revenue, allowing businesses to align their financing obligations with their cash flow.

One of the key advantages of merchant financing is its simplicity and convenience compared to traditional forms of financing. Since repayment is based on a percentage of revenue, rather than a fixed amount, businesses can adjust their repayment obligations based on their sales volume, allowing them to manage cash flow more effectively. Additionally, merchant financing does not require businesses to provide collateral or undergo a lengthy approval process, making it an attractive option for businesses with limited assets or credit history.

Leveraging Target Company Assets and Cash Reserves

In addition to external financing options, buyers can leverage the assets and cash reserves of the target company to finance an LBO. This approach allows buyers to reduce their reliance on external debt or equity financing and preserve financial flexibility.

Using Target Company Assets as Collateral

Buyers can leverage the assets of the target company, such as accounts receivable, inventory, equipment, real estate, or intellectual property, as collateral for financing arrangements. By pledging these assets as security, buyers can secure loans or lines of credit from lenders, using the value of the assets to support the borrowing.

Using target company assets as collateral provides buyers with access to financing at favorable terms, as lenders are more willing to extend credit when the loan is secured by tangible assets. Additionally, using target company assets as collateral can reduce the cost of financing, as lenders may offer lower interest rates or fees in exchange for the additional security provided by the assets.

Utilizing Target Company Cash Reserves

Buyers can also leverage the cash reserves of the target company to finance a portion of the acquisition price or cover transaction-related expenses. Target companies may accumulate cash reserves over time through profitable operations, prudent financial management, or capital injections from investors.

Utilizing target company cash reserves provides buyers with immediate access to capital without the need for external financing, reducing reliance on debt and preserving financial flexibility. However, buyers should carefully assess the impact of using target company cash reserves on the company's liquidity, financial stability, and future growth prospects.

Conclusion

Deal structure and financing are critical aspects of a leveraged buyout (LBO) transaction that require careful consideration and planning. By exploring different financing options, including asset-based lending, invoice financing, and merchant financing, buyers can access the capital needed to fund acquisitions and support growth initiatives. Additionally, leveraging target company assets and cash reserves can provide buyers with alternative sources of financing and reduce reliance on external debt. Ultimately, selecting the right financing strategy is essential for maximizing value, mitigating risk, and achieving long-term success in an LBO transaction.

Chapter 10: Positioning Yourself as a Buyer

Positioning yourself effectively as a buyer in the context of leveraged buyouts (LBOs) is crucial for gaining credibility, building trust with sellers, and ultimately securing successful deals. This chapter explores strategies for establishing a strong presence in the market, demonstrating expertise and experience, and creating a professional image that inspires confidence in potential sellers.

Building a Strong Personal Brand
Defining Your Unique Value Proposition

Defining your unique value proposition as a buyer is essential for distinguishing yourself in a competitive market. Your value proposition should encapsulate what makes you stand out from other buyers and why sellers should choose to do business with you. Consider your strengths, skills, experience, and track record when crafting your value proposition. Are you known for your strategic vision, operational expertise, financial acumen, or industry connections? Identifying and articulating these qualities will help you communicate your value effectively to potential sellers.

Once you've defined your value proposition, ensure that it aligns with the needs and preferences of your target sellers. Consider what sellers are looking for in a buyer and tailor your value proposition accordingly. For example, if you specialize in turning around distressed companies, emphasize your ability to revitalize struggling businesses and unlock their potential. If you have a strong track record of growing companies in a specific industry, highlight your industry expertise and success stories.

Establishing an Online Presence

In today's digital age, an online presence is essential for building credibility and visibility as a buyer. Potential sellers are likely to research you online before engaging in discussions, so it's important to have a professional and polished presence on relevant platforms. Start by creating a LinkedIn profile that showcases your experience, expertise, and accomplishments. Use a professional photo and write a compelling summary that highlights your value proposition and key achievements.

In addition to LinkedIn, consider establishing a presence on other platforms where potential sellers may be active, such as industry-specific forums, social media groups, or online marketplaces. Share relevant content, engage with industry thought leaders, and participate in discussions to demonstrate your expertise and establish yourself as a credible authority in your field.

Cultivating Relationships and Networks

Building relationships and networks within the industry is critical for gaining access to deal flow and building trust with potential sellers. Networking events, industry conferences, and professional associations are valuable opportunities to connect with other professionals in your field and expand your network. Take the time to build genuine relationships with other industry professionals, including lawyers, accountants, investment bankers, and business owners. These relationships can provide valuable insights, referrals, and support throughout the deal-making process.

Networking is not just about making connections; it's about nurturing and maintaining relationships over time. Stay in touch with your contacts, share relevant information and resources, and offer assistance whenever possible. By cultivating strong relationships within the industry, you'll increase your visibility, credibility, and ultimately, your chances of success as a buyer.

Demonstrating Expertise and Experience
Showcasing Past Successes

One of the most effective ways to demonstrate expertise and experience as a buyer is to showcase your track record of successful deals. Highlight past successes, case studies, and testimonials from satisfied clients to illustrate your ability to execute transactions and deliver results. Provide concrete examples of deals you've completed, including the size, industry, and outcomes achieved. For example, you could share stories of how you identified and capitalized on growth opportunities, navigated complex negotiations, or successfully integrated acquired businesses.

In addition to highlighting your successes, be transparent about your failures and setbacks. Discuss how you've learned from past experiences and used them to inform your approach to future deals. Authenticity and humility can go a long way in building trust with potential sellers and demonstrating your commitment to continuous improvement and growth.

Communicating Industry Knowledge

Demonstrating a deep understanding of the industry and market dynamics is essential for building confidence with potential sellers. Stay informed about industry trends, competitive landscapes, and regulatory developments that may impact the businesses you are targeting. Share insights and perspectives on market conditions, opportunities, and challenges to demonstrate your expertise and credibility as a buyer.

Consider publishing articles, whitepapers, or blog posts on relevant topics within your industry. Offer thought leadership and strategic insights that provide value to potential sellers and position you as a trusted advisor and partner. By demonstrating your knowledge and expertise, you'll differentiate yourself from other buyers and build confidence with potential sellers.

Offering Value-Added Services

Differentiate yourself as a buyer by offering value-added services that go beyond the traditional transaction process. Consider how you can add value to potential sellers before, during, and after the deal. For example, you could provide strategic advice, operational expertise, or access to a network of industry contacts that can help sellers maximize the value of their businesses.

During the due diligence process, look for opportunities to identify and address potential risks or challenges that could impact the success of the deal. Offer recommendations and solutions based on your expertise and experience to help sellers mitigate risks and maximize value. After the deal closes, continue to provide support and guidance to sellers as they navigate the transition and integration process. By demonstrating your commitment to adding value beyond the transaction, you'll build trust and credibility with potential sellers and increase your chances of success as a buyer.

Creating a Professional Image
Presenting Yourself Professionally

Creating a professional image begins with presenting yourself professionally in all interactions with potential sellers and stakeholders. Pay attention to your appearance, demeanor, and communication style to convey professionalism and credibility. Dress appropriately for meetings and presentations, and ensure that your appearance reflects the seriousness and importance of the discussions. Communicate clearly and confidently, using language that is professional and respectful. Be punctual, reliable, and responsive in all communications and interactions, demonstrating your commitment to professionalism and excellence.

Building a Strong Team

Surrounding yourself with a strong team of professionals is essential for positioning yourself as a credible buyer. Your team should include experts with diverse skills and experiences, such as lawyers, accountants, financial advisors, and industry specialists. Each member of your team should bring unique insights and capabilities that complement your own, allowing you to offer comprehensive support and guidance to potential sellers throughout the deal-making process.

When assembling your team, look for professionals who are not only highly skilled and knowledgeable but also trustworthy and reliable. Building a strong team is not just about individual expertise; it's about collaboration, communication, and mutual respect. Foster a culture of teamwork and cooperation, where everyone works together towards a common goal of achieving success for your clients and stakeholders.

Leveraging Professional Materials

Investing in professional materials is another important aspect of creating a professional image as a buyer. Ensure that your business cards, presentation decks, and marketing materials are well-designed, informative, and aligned with your brand identity. Your materials should reflect the quality and professionalism of your services, conveying confidence and credibility to potential sellers.

When designing your materials, pay attention to details such as branding, messaging, and visual appeal. Use high-quality images, graphics, and typography to enhance the visual impact of your materials and make them more engaging and memorable. Tailor your materials to the needs and interests of potential sellers, focusing on the value you can offer and the benefits of working with you as a buyer.

Conclusion

Positioning yourself as a buyer in the context of leveraged buyouts (LBOs) requires a strategic and thoughtful approach. By building a strong personal brand, demonstrating expertise and experience, and creating a professional image, you can differentiate yourself from other buyers and build credibility and trust with potential sellers. Invest time and effort in defining your unique value proposition, establishing an online presence, and cultivating relationships and networks within the industry. Showcase your track record of success, communicate your industry knowledge, and offer value-added services that set you apart from the competition. Present yourself professionally in all interactions, build a strong team of professionals, and invest in high-quality materials that reflect the quality and professionalism of your services. By following these strategies, you can position yourself as a trusted and credible buyer, increase your visibility and credibility, and ultimately, secure successful deals in the competitive LBO market.

Chapter 11: Heads of Terms/LOI

Heads of Terms, also known as Letters of Intent (LOIs), are preliminary documents that outline the key terms and conditions of a potential deal. This chapter delves into the importance of understanding these key terms and conditions and provides guidance on drafting effective Heads of Terms or LOIs.

Understanding Key Terms and Conditions

Purchase Price and Payment Terms

The purchase price and payment terms are arguably the most critical aspects of any deal outlined in the Heads of Terms (HOT) or Letter of Intent (LOI). This section sets the foundation for the financial transaction, dictating how much the buyer will pay for the acquisition and how and when those payments will be made.

In negotiating the purchase price, the buyer and seller must consider various factors, including the company's financial performance, market conditions, growth prospects, and potential synergies. The payment terms may include upfront payments, installments, earn-outs, or other contingent payments based on future performance metrics. It's crucial to clearly specify the form and timing of payments to avoid misunderstandings and disputes later in the transaction process.

Deal Structure and Transaction Mechanics

The deal structure outlined in the HOT or LOI defines how the transaction will be executed, whether it's structured as a stock purchase, asset purchase, merger, or another form of transaction. This section also outlines the key steps and milestones involved in completing the transaction, including due diligence, regulatory approvals, financing arrangements, and the timeline for closing.

The parties must carefully consider the implications of the chosen deal structure on taxes, liabilities, and other legal and financial aspects of the transaction. For example, a stock purchase may result in different tax consequences for the buyer and seller compared to an asset purchase. By clearly outlining the transaction mechanics in the HOT or LOI, the parties can align their expectations and facilitate a smoother transaction process.

Due Diligence and Conditions Precedent

Due diligence is a critical stage in the transaction process, allowing the buyer to evaluate the target company's operations, finances, legal compliance, and other key aspects before completing the acquisition. The HOT or LOI should specify the scope and timing of the due diligence process, including access to information, cooperation from the seller, and any limitations or exclusions.

Additionally, the HOT or LOI may include conditions precedent that must be satisfied before the transaction can proceed, such as obtaining regulatory approvals, securing financing, or obtaining third-party consents. These conditions help protect the buyer's interests and ensure that the transaction is feasible and legally permissible. By clearly outlining the due diligence process and conditions precedent in the HOT or LOI, the parties can manage expectations and mitigate risks throughout the transaction process.

Representations, Warranties, and Indemnities

Representations, warranties, and indemnities are contractual provisions that allocate risk between the buyer and seller in a transaction. The seller typically makes representations and warranties regarding the target company's operations, financial condition, legal compliance, and other relevant matters. These representations and warranties serve as assurances to the buyer regarding the accuracy and completeness of the information provided.

In the event that a representation or warranty is breached, the buyer may be entitled to indemnification from the seller to compensate for any losses or damages incurred as a result. The HOT or LOI should specify the scope and limitations of indemnification, including any caps, baskets, survival periods, or other terms that govern the parties' liability.

Confidentiality and Exclusivity

Confidentiality and exclusivity provisions are designed to protect the parties' sensitive information and ensure that negotiations remain confidential and exclusive. The HOT or LOI may include provisions requiring the parties to maintain the confidentiality of information exchanged during the negotiation process and prohibiting them from disclosing or using that information for any purpose other than evaluating the proposed transaction.

Additionally, the HOT or LOI may grant the buyer a period of exclusivity during which the seller agrees not to solicit or entertain offers from other potential buyers. Exclusivity periods provide the buyer with time to conduct due diligence, negotiate definitive agreements, and secure financing without the risk of competing offers emerging.

Drafting Effective Heads of Terms/LOI

Clarity and Specificity

When drafting a HOT or LOI, clarity and specificity are essential to ensure that the document accurately reflects the parties' intentions and expectations. Clearly outline each key term and condition of the proposed deal in a straightforward and unambiguous manner. Avoid vague or ambiguous language that could lead to misunderstandings or disputes down the line. Be specific about each party's rights, obligations, and expectations to facilitate a smooth and efficient transaction process.

Flexibility and Contingencies

While it's crucial to be specific about the key terms and conditions of the deal, it's also important to build in flexibility and contingencies to accommodate unforeseen circumstances or developments. Include provisions that allow for adjustments to the purchase price or payment terms based on the outcome of due diligence or other factors. Consider including provisions that address potential deal breakers or deal killers, such as regulatory approvals, financing contingencies, or material adverse changes. By incorporating flexibility and contingencies into the HOT or LOI, the parties can adapt to changing circumstances and minimize the risk of deal failure.

Collaboration and Cooperation

Drafting a HOT or LOI should be a collaborative process that involves input from both parties. Engage in open and constructive discussions with the seller to negotiate mutually acceptable terms and conditions. Be prepared to compromise and find creative solutions to overcome any obstacles or disagreements that may arise. By working together in good faith, the parties can lay the foundation for a successful transaction and build a positive relationship with each other. Collaboration and cooperation are essential throughout the negotiation process, from drafting the initial HOT or LOI to finalizing the definitive agreements and closing the deal.

Legal Review and Approval

Finally, it's essential to have the HOT or LOI reviewed and approved by legal counsel before finalizing and executing the document. Legal counsel can help ensure that the document accurately reflects the parties' intentions, complies with applicable laws and regulations, and protects the parties' interests. They can also advise on any potential legal risks or pitfalls and help negotiate any contentious issues or sticking points. By involving legal counsel early in the process, the parties can avoid costly mistakes and ensure that the HOT or LOI effectively captures the terms and conditions of the proposed transaction.

Conclusion

Heads of Terms and Letters of Intent are critical documents in the deal-making process, providing a framework for negotiating and finalizing the terms and conditions of a potential transaction. By understanding the key terms and conditions and drafting effective

HOTs or LOIs that accurately reflect the parties' intentions, the parties can lay the groundwork for a successful transaction and minimize the risk of misunderstandings or disputes. Clarity, specificity, flexibility, and collaboration are essential elements of drafting effective HOTs or LOIs. By incorporating these principles and involving legal counsel in the review and approval process, the parties can negotiate and finalize a document that sets the stage for a successful transaction.

In summary, Heads of Terms and Letters of Intent serve as important preliminary documents in the M&A process, outlining the key terms and conditions of a potential deal. Understanding the significance of each aspect, such as purchase price, deal structure, due diligence, representations, and confidentiality, is crucial for both buyers and sellers. Moreover, drafting effective HOTs or LOIs requires clarity, specificity, flexibility, and collaboration to ensure that the document accurately reflects the parties' intentions and expectations. By following these principles and involving legal counsel in the review process, the parties can navigate the negotiation process more smoothly and increase the likelihood of a successful transaction.

Chapter 12: Due Diligence Process

The due diligence process is a critical stage in the M&A journey, providing the buyer with an opportunity to conduct a comprehensive review of the target company's operations, finances, legal standing, and other key aspects. This chapter explores the various components of the due diligence process, emphasizing the importance of thorough analysis and evaluation.

Conducting Thorough Financial Analysis

Financial analysis lies at the heart of the due diligence process in mergers and acquisitions (M&A). It involves scrutinizing the target company's financial statements, records, and performance to assess its financial health, stability, and potential for growth. Here's a detailed exploration of each component of financial analysis:

Reviewing Financial Statements

The review of financial statements encompasses analyzing the income statement, balance sheet, and cash flow statement. These documents provide a snapshot of the target company's financial performance over a specific period, typically the last three to five years. By examining trends in revenue, expenses, assets, liabilities, and cash flows, the buyer gains insights into the company's profitability, liquidity, and solvency.

Analyzing Financial Performance

Analyzing financial performance goes beyond merely reviewing historical financials. It involves delving deeper into key financial metrics and ratios to assess the company's efficiency, profitability, and financial stability. Metrics such as gross margin, operating margin, return on assets (ROA), return on equity (ROE), and debt-to-equity ratio provide valuable insights into the company's operational efficiency, profitability, and leverage. Benchmarking these metrics against industry peers helps evaluate the company's relative performance and identify areas for improvement.

Identifying Risks and Opportunities

Financial analysis is not just about evaluating past performance; it's also about identifying potential risks and opportunities that may impact the company's future prospects. Risks such as declining revenue, increasing costs, high debt levels, or dependence on a single customer or supplier can pose significant challenges post-acquisition. Conversely, opportunities such as untapped markets, innovative products, or operational efficiencies can drive value creation and growth. By conducting a thorough analysis of risks and opportunities, the buyer can make informed decisions and develop strategies to mitigate risks and capitalize on opportunities.

Assessing Legal, Regulatory, and Compliance Issues

In addition to financial analysis, due diligence involves assessing the legal, regulatory, and compliance landscape to identify any potential risks or liabilities that may impact the target company's operations or financial standing. Here's a detailed exploration of each aspect:

Reviewing Legal Documentation

The review of legal documentation involves examining contracts, agreements, licenses, permits, and other legal instruments that govern the target company's operations and relationships. This includes customer contracts, supplier agreements, lease agreements, employment contracts, intellectual property licenses, and any other agreements that may impact the company's rights, obligations, or liabilities. The goal is to identify any material legal risks, obligations, or contingencies that may pose challenges post-acquisition.

Evaluating Regulatory Compliance

Ensuring compliance with applicable laws, regulations, and industry standards is critical for mitigating legal and regulatory risks. The buyer conducts a thorough review of the target company's compliance practices and procedures, including environmental, health and safety regulations, data privacy laws, employment laws, and industry-specific regulations. Any non-compliance issues or regulatory violations must be identified, assessed, and addressed to avoid potential fines, penalties, or legal liabilities post-acquisition.

Assessing Litigation and Legal Risks

Litigation and legal risks can have significant implications for the target company's financial and operational performance. The buyer evaluates any pending or potential litigation, claims, or disputes involving the target company, including their potential impact on the company's reputation, finances, and operations. Legal counsel may be engaged to assess the merits of any legal claims and advise on the potential liabilities and costs associated with resolving them. By identifying and addressing litigation and legal risks early in the due diligence process, the buyer can mitigate potential legal liabilities and ensure a smoother transition post-acquisition.

Evaluating Operational and Strategic Fit

Assessing the operational and strategic fit between the buyer and the target company is essential for determining the potential synergies and value creation opportunities associated with the acquisition. Here's a detailed exploration of each aspect:

Assessing Operational Efficiency

Operational efficiency is a key determinant of the target company's ability to generate value and sustain growth. The buyer evaluates the target company's operational performance, including production efficiency, supply chain management, inventory management, and quality control processes. By identifying areas of inefficiency or bottlenecks, the buyer can develop strategies to optimize operations post-acquisition and drive value creation.

Evaluating Strategic Alignment

Strategic alignment between the buyer and the target company is critical for realizing synergies and achieving strategic objectives. The buyer evaluates factors such as market positioning, product portfolios, distribution channels, and customer base to assess the degree of strategic fit between the two entities. By aligning their strategic priorities and capabilities, the buyer and the target company can leverage complementary strengths and resources to drive growth, innovation, and competitive advantage in the marketplace.

Identifying Integration Risks and Opportunities

Integration planning begins during the due diligence process, as the buyer identifies potential integration risks and opportunities associated with combining the target company with its existing operations. This includes assessing cultural differences, organizational structures, IT systems, and processes to develop a comprehensive integration plan that minimizes disruptions and maximizes value creation post-acquisition. By addressing integration challenges proactively during due diligence, the buyer can accelerate the integration process and realize synergies more effectively.

Conclusion

In conclusion, the due diligence process is a multifaceted endeavor that involves conducting thorough financial analysis, assessing legal, regulatory, and compliance issues, and evaluating operational and strategic fit. By analyzing financial performance, identifying risks and opportunities, reviewing legal documentation, evaluating regulatory compliance, assessing operational efficiency, evaluating strategic alignment, and identifying integration risks and opportunities, the buyer can gain a comprehensive understanding of the target company and make informed decisions about the potential acquisition. Effective due diligence lays the foundation for a successful transaction and sets the stage for value creation and growth post-acquisition.

Chapter 13: Contract Negotiation and Drafting

Contract negotiation and drafting are critical components of the M&A process, as they formalize the terms and conditions of the transaction and establish the rights and obligations of the parties involved. This chapter explores the key considerations and best practices for navigating the negotiation and drafting of M&A contracts.

Working with Legal Professionals
Legal Expertise and Guidance

Legal professionals play a pivotal role in the M&A process, offering specialized expertise and guidance to navigate the complexities of contract negotiation and drafting. Their knowledge of corporate law, M&A regulations, and industry practices enables them to provide valuable insights and advice to their clients. By understanding the legal implications of various contract terms and structures, legal professionals help their clients make informed decisions and mitigate legal risks.

In the context of contract negotiation, legal professionals work closely with their clients to understand their objectives, priorities, and concerns. They analyze the deal dynamics, assess the legal implications of proposed terms, and develop strategies to achieve favorable outcomes. By collaborating with their clients and other stakeholders, legal professionals ensure that the contract terms align with the parties' intentions and objectives while also complying with relevant laws and regulations.

Collaborative Approach

Effective contract negotiation requires a collaborative approach involving the buyer, seller, and their respective legal teams. Legal professionals work as trusted advisors to their clients, facilitating open communication and collaboration throughout the negotiation process. They act as advocates for their clients' interests while also seeking to achieve a mutually beneficial outcome for all parties involved.

Collaboration extends beyond the negotiation table, as legal professionals coordinate with other advisors, such as financial advisors, tax experts, and industry specialists, to address multifaceted issues and develop comprehensive solutions. By leveraging the collective expertise of diverse stakeholders, legal professionals ensure that the contract terms reflect a thorough analysis of the transaction's legal, financial, and operational aspects.

Due Diligence Review

A crucial aspect of working with legal professionals in contract negotiation is the due diligence review. Legal professionals conduct a comprehensive review of due diligence findings to identify any legal, regulatory, or compliance issues that may impact the contract terms. This involves examining the target company's legal documentation, contracts, agreements, permits, and licenses to assess their validity, enforceability, and compliance with applicable laws and regulations.

During the due diligence review, legal professionals collaborate with other advisors to evaluate the legal implications of various aspects of the transaction, such as intellectual property rights, employment agreements, environmental regulations, and litigation risks. Any material legal risks or contingencies identified during due diligence are addressed in the contract negotiation process to mitigate potential liabilities and ensure legal compliance.

Ensuring Clarity and Legal Compliance
Clear and Precise Language

Clarity and precision in contract drafting are essential to minimize the risk of misunderstandings or disputes. Legal professionals carefully craft the contract terms using clear, precise, and unambiguous language that accurately reflects the parties' intentions and expectations. They avoid using overly technical or obscure language that may be open to interpretation, opting instead for straightforward and understandable language that facilitates clarity and comprehension.

Clear and precise language not only helps to ensure that the contract terms are accurately understood by all parties but also facilitates smoother implementation and enforcement of the contract terms. By eliminating ambiguity and confusion, legal professionals reduce the likelihood of disputes arising during the performance of the contract and enhance the parties' ability to enforce their rights and obligations effectively.

Compliance with Applicable Laws

Contracts must comply with applicable laws, regulations, and industry standards to ensure legal validity and enforceability. Legal professionals stay abreast of the latest legal developments and regulatory requirements relevant to the transaction, advising their clients on compliance obligations and best practices. They conduct a thorough analysis of the legal landscape to identify any legal risks or regulatory requirements that may impact the contract terms.

During contract drafting, legal professionals tailor the contract terms to address specific legal requirements and mitigate legal risks. They incorporate provisions that ensure compliance with relevant laws and regulations, such as anti-corruption laws, data privacy regulations, intellectual property rights, and environmental regulations. By proactively addressing legal compliance issues in the contract, legal professionals help their clients avoid potential fines, penalties, or legal liabilities post-acquisition.

Risk Allocation and Mitigation

Contracts allocate risks and liabilities between the parties in a manner that is fair, reasonable, and consistent with their respective bargaining power and interests. Legal professionals assess the allocation of risks and liabilities based on due diligence findings, negotiation priorities, and industry norms. They advise their clients on risk mitigation strategies and contractual protections to minimize potential risks and liabilities.

Provisions such as indemnification, limitations of liability, representations and warranties, and dispute resolution mechanisms are carefully negotiated to balance the parties' interests and allocate risks appropriately. Legal professionals work with their clients to identify potential areas of exposure and develop strategies to mitigate risks effectively. By addressing risk allocation and mitigation in the contract, legal professionals help their clients navigate the transaction with confidence and minimize the risk of disputes or legal challenges post-acquisition.

Conclusion

In conclusion, working with legal professionals is essential for navigating the complexities of contract negotiation and drafting in M&A transactions. Legal professionals offer valuable expertise and guidance to their clients, ensuring that the contract terms align with the parties' intentions and objectives while also complying with relevant laws and regulations. By adopting a collaborative approach, conducting a thorough due diligence review, ensuring clarity and legal compliance, and addressing risk allocation and mitigation, legal professionals help their clients negotiate and draft contracts that facilitate successful transactions and minimize legal risks. Effective collaboration between legal professionals and their clients is critical for achieving favorable outcomes and ensuring the long-term success of M&A transactions.

Chapter 14: Closing the Deal

Closing the deal marks the culmination of the M&A process, as the parties finalize the legal and financial aspects of the transaction and formally transfer ownership of the target company. This chapter explores the key steps and considerations involved in closing the deal, from finalizing legal and financial documents to celebrating successful completion.

Finalizing Legal and Financial Documents
Definitive Agreements

Finalizing legal and financial documents is a critical aspect of closing the deal in an M&A transaction. At the heart of this process are the definitive agreements, which formalize the terms and conditions of the deal between the buyer and the seller. These agreements typically include the purchase agreement, shareholder agreements (if applicable), and any ancillary documents necessary to complete the transaction.

The purchase agreement is the central document that governs the transaction and outlines key terms such as the purchase price, payment terms, representations and warranties, indemnification provisions, closing conditions, and post-closing obligations. Legal professionals play a crucial role in drafting and negotiating the purchase agreement to ensure that it accurately reflects the parties' intentions, protects their interests, and mitigates potential risks.

In addition to the purchase agreement, other ancillary documents may be required depending on the specifics of the transaction. These may include employment agreements, non-compete agreements, transition services agreements, intellectual property assignments, and any other agreements necessary to effectuate the transfer of ownership and ensure the smooth transition of the target company to the buyer.

Regulatory Approvals

In many M&A transactions, obtaining regulatory approvals is a key requirement for closing the deal. Depending on the nature of the transaction and the industries involved, regulatory approvals may be necessary to ensure compliance with antitrust laws, competition regulations, industry-specific regulations, or other legal requirements.

Legal professionals work closely with regulatory agencies and governmental authorities to identify any required approvals and oversee the preparation and submission of necessary filings. This may involve conducting pre-filing consultations, preparing comprehensive submissions, responding to inquiries from regulatory authorities, and addressing any concerns or objections raised during the review process.

Obtaining regulatory approvals can be a complex and time-consuming process, requiring careful coordination and collaboration between the parties involved. Legal professionals play a crucial role in navigating the regulatory landscape, ensuring compliance with applicable laws and regulations, and facilitating the timely completion of the transaction.

Closing Conditions

Before closing the deal, the parties must satisfy all closing conditions specified in the definitive agreements. These closing conditions are typically outlined in the purchase agreement and may include various requirements such as obtaining financing commitments, securing third-party consents, completing due diligence investigations, resolving outstanding legal or regulatory issues, and fulfilling any other contractual obligations.

Legal professionals work diligently to ensure that all closing conditions are met and facilitate a smooth and timely closing process. This may involve coordinating with various stakeholders, conducting additional due diligence or negotiations as necessary, and addressing any outstanding issues or concerns that may arise during the closing process.

By ensuring that all closing conditions are satisfied, legal professionals help minimize the risk of delays or complications and ensure that the transaction proceeds according to plan. Their expertise and attention to detail are essential for navigating the complexities of the closing process and facilitating a successful outcome for all parties involved.

Celebrating Successful Completion
Closing Ceremony

The closing ceremony is a symbolic event that marks the formal completion of the M&A transaction. It typically involves the exchange of signed documents, payment of the purchase price, and transfer of ownership of the target company from the seller to the buyer. The closing ceremony may take place in person or remotely, depending on the preferences and logistical considerations of the parties involved.

Legal professionals, along with other advisors and stakeholders, may participate in the closing ceremony to witness the formalization of the deal and celebrate the achievement of a significant milestone. This provides an opportunity to acknowledge the collective effort and collaboration that went into completing the transaction and to express gratitude to everyone who contributed to its success.

Post-Closing Obligations

Following the closing of the deal, the parties may have certain post-closing obligations to fulfill. These may include making post-closing adjustments to the purchase price, transferring licenses and permits, integrating operations, or addressing any remaining legal or regulatory issues. Legal professionals continue to provide guidance and support to their clients during the post-closing phase, ensuring that all post-closing obligations are met and any remaining issues are resolved promptly and effectively.

Legal professionals play a crucial role in facilitating the smooth transition of ownership and ensuring that all post-closing obligations are fulfilled in accordance with the terms of the definitive agreements. This may involve coordinating with various stakeholders, preparing and executing additional documentation, and addressing any unforeseen challenges or issues that may arise during the post-closing period.

Celebrating Success

Closing the deal is a momentous occasion that warrants celebration and recognition of the hard work, dedication, and collaboration that went into completing the transaction. The parties involved, including the buyer, seller, advisors, and other stakeholders, may organize a closing celebration or toast to commemorate the successful completion of the deal. This provides an opportunity to reflect on the journey, acknowledge achievements, and express gratitude to everyone who contributed to the success of the transaction.

Legal professionals often play a behind-the-scenes role in facilitating the closing process, but their contributions are essential to the successful completion of the transaction. By ensuring compliance with legal requirements, facilitating negotiations, and addressing any legal or regulatory issues that may arise, legal professionals help pave the way for a smooth and successful closing. Their expertise, diligence, and attention to detail are instrumental in navigating the complexities of the closing process and achieving a positive outcome for all parties involved.

Conclusion and Handover

Once all legal and financial documents have been finalized, closing conditions have been satisfied, and post-closing obligations have been fulfilled, the transaction is officially closed. Legal professionals oversee the finalization of paperwork, including the execution of documents, transfer of funds, and completion of any remaining administrative tasks.

During this phase, legal professionals ensure that all necessary paperwork is properly executed and filed with the relevant authorities to formalize the transfer of ownership and ensure compliance with legal and regulatory requirements. This may include updating corporate records, notifying regulatory agencies of the change in ownership, and recording the transaction with relevant government authorities.

Following the completion of all closing activities, legal professionals formally hand over control of the target company to the buyer. This may involve providing the buyer with copies of all executed documents, transferring access to key assets and information, and facilitating the transition of responsibilities from the seller to the buyer.

Post-Closing Review and Evaluation

After the deal is closed, legal professionals may conduct a post-closing review and evaluation to assess the overall effectiveness of the closing process and identify any lessons learned or areas for improvement. This may involve soliciting feedback from the parties involved, evaluating the efficiency of the closing process, and identifying any issues or challenges that arose during the transaction.

The post-closing review provides an opportunity to reflect on the transaction, celebrate successes, and identify opportunities for continuous improvement. Legal professionals play a key role in facilitating this process, providing insights and recommendations based on their experience and expertise.

Continuing Relationship

While the formal transaction may be complete, the relationship between the parties often continues beyond the closing of the deal. Legal professionals may continue to provide support and guidance to their clients as they navigate the post-acquisition integration process, address any remaining legal or regulatory issues, and pursue opportunities for growth and expansion.

By maintaining ongoing communication and collaboration with their clients, legal professionals can help ensure a smooth transition and facilitate a successful long-term relationship between the buyer and the seller. This may involve providing advice on post-closing matters, assisting with the resolution of any disputes or issues that may arise, and helping to identify opportunities for collaboration and synergy between the parties.

Conclusion

Closing the deal is a significant milestone in the M&A process, representing the formal completion of the transaction and the beginning of a new chapter for the parties involved. By finalizing legal and financial documents, satisfying closing conditions, and celebrating successful completion, the parties formalize the transfer of ownership of the target company and set the stage for integration and future growth.

Legal professionals play a crucial role in guiding their clients through the closing process, ensuring compliance with legal and regulatory requirements, and facilitating a smooth and timely closing. Through collaboration, diligence, and attention to detail, legal professionals help ensure a successful outcome for all parties involved and lay the foundation for a successful long-term relationship between the buyer and the seller.

Chapter 15: Post-Acquisition Management

Post-acquisition management is a critical phase in the M&A process, where the focus shifts from deal-making to integration and value creation. This chapter delves into the key aspects of post-acquisition management, including the first 90 days of integration and transition, implementing growth strategies, and monitoring performance to ensure the success of the acquisition.

The First 90 Days: Integration and Transition

Integration Planning

The first 90 days following an acquisition are often referred to as the "honeymoon period," a critical time when the initial excitement of the deal gives way to the hard work of integration. Integration planning begins well before the deal closes, as companies conduct due diligence to identify synergies, risks, and opportunities for integration. However, it's during the first 90 days post-closing that the integration plan is put into action.

Integration planning involves developing a roadmap that outlines the steps, timelines, and responsibilities for merging the two organizations. This plan typically covers various aspects of integration, including organizational structure, culture integration, technology systems, processes, and people. A well-developed integration plan serves as a guiding framework for the integration team, ensuring that efforts are coordinated, focused, and aligned with the strategic objectives of the deal.

Cultural Integration

One of the most challenging aspects of post-acquisition integration is cultural integration. Cultural differences between the buyer and the target company can create significant hurdles to effective integration, impacting employee morale, productivity, and ultimately, the success of the deal. Therefore, it's essential for leaders to prioritize cultural integration from the outset and foster an inclusive and collaborative work environment.

Leaders play a critical role in bridging cultural gaps, fostering open communication, and promoting a sense of unity and shared purpose among employees. They must lead by example, embodying the values and behaviors they want to see in the combined organization. By creating opportunities for employees to connect, collaborate, and build relationships across organizational boundaries, leaders can help break down cultural barriers and create a cohesive and high-performing culture.

Talent Retention

Employee retention is another key consideration during the integration phase. The uncertainty and change associated with mergers and acquisitions can create anxiety and fear among employees, leading to talent attrition. To mitigate this risk, leaders must focus on engaging employees, providing clarity and transparency about the integration process, and recognizing and rewarding top performers.

Leadership development programs, training initiatives, and career advancement opportunities can help retain key talent and foster a culture of growth and development within the organization. By investing in their people and demonstrating a commitment to their success, leaders can build trust and loyalty among employees and position the organization for long-term success.

Implementing Growth Strategies

Synergy Realization

One of the primary objectives of an acquisition is to realize synergies that create value for the combined organization. Synergies may arise from cost savings, revenue enhancements, or strategic advantages gained through the combination of complementary resources, capabilities, and market positions. However, capturing synergies requires careful planning, execution, and coordination across the organization.

Leaders must identify and prioritize synergies early in the integration process and develop actionable plans to capture them. This may involve consolidating operations, streamlining processes, cross-selling products or services, leveraging economies of scale, or entering new markets. By effectively capturing synergies, leaders can enhance the competitiveness and profitability of the combined organization and maximize shareholder value.

Market Expansion

Acquisitions provide an opportunity for the buyer to expand its market presence and reach new customers, geographies, or market segments. Leaders must develop strategies to capitalize on these opportunities and drive growth through market expansion initiatives.

This may involve leveraging the target company's customer relationships, distribution channels, or brand equity to penetrate new markets or diversify revenue streams. Leaders may also explore opportunities for product or service innovation, strategic partnerships, or acquisitions to further accelerate growth and strengthen the organization's competitive position in the marketplace.

Monitoring Performance and Adjusting Strategies
Performance Metrics

Monitoring performance is essential for assessing the effectiveness of post-acquisition strategies and identifying areas for improvement. Leaders must establish key performance indicators (KPIs) and metrics to track progress against strategic objectives and measure the impact of integration efforts on financial and operational performance.

Performance metrics may include revenue growth, profit margins, market share, customer satisfaction, employee engagement, and other indicators relevant to the organization's goals and objectives. By regularly reviewing and analyzing performance data, leaders can identify trends, opportunities, and challenges and make informed decisions to drive continuous improvement and achieve sustainable growth.

Agility and Flexibility

In a dynamic and uncertain business environment, leaders must remain agile and adaptable in their approach to post-acquisition management. This may require adjusting strategies, reallocating resources, or pivoting to new opportunities in response to changing market conditions, competitive pressures, or unforeseen challenges.

Leaders must foster a culture of innovation, experimentation, and continuous learning within the organization to encourage creativity and resilience in the face of uncertainty. By embracing change and maintaining a flexible mindset, leaders can position the organization to thrive in an ever-evolving marketplace and capitalize on emerging opportunities for growth and expansion.

Conclusion

Post-acquisition management is a multifaceted process that requires careful planning, execution, and monitoring to ensure the success of the acquisition. By focusing on integration and transition during the first 90 days, implementing growth strategies to capitalize on synergies and market opportunities, and monitoring performance to adjust strategies as needed, leaders can position the organization for long-term success and create sustainable value for shareholders, employees, and other stakeholders.

Effective post-acquisition management requires strong leadership, clear communication, and a commitment to collaboration and continuous improvement. By investing in their people, leveraging synergies, and remaining agile and adaptable in their approach, leaders can navigate the complexities of post-acquisition integration and drive growth and innovation to achieve strategic objectives and create a competitive advantage in the marketplace.

Chapter 16: Special Purpose Vehicles (SPVs)

Special Purpose Vehicles (SPVs), also known as Special Purpose Entities (SPEs) or Special Purpose Companies (SPCs), are legal entities created for a specific, often limited, purpose. This chapter explores the purpose, structure, benefits, and considerations of SPVs in the context of mergers and acquisitions and other financial transactions.

Understanding the Purpose and Structure
Purpose of SPVs

Special Purpose Vehicles (SPVs) serve a variety of purposes in the financial landscape, offering companies a flexible and efficient way to achieve specific objectives. One primary purpose of SPVs is risk isolation. By creating a separate legal entity, companies can isolate and contain financial risk associated with particular assets or liabilities. This risk isolation serves to protect the sponsoring company's other assets from potential losses, providing a layer of security and stability.

Another common purpose of SPVs is securitization. In securitization transactions, financial assets such as loans, mortgages, or receivables are pooled together and packaged into tradable securities. These securities are then sold to investors, providing liquidity and funding for the originating institution. SPVs play a crucial role in securitization by acting as the legal entity through which the assets are held and managed, ensuring compliance with regulatory requirements and providing a clear legal framework for investors.

Additionally, SPVs may be structured to achieve specific tax benefits. Companies may utilize SPVs to minimize tax liabilities or access favorable tax treatment for certain types of transactions. By structuring transactions through an SPV, companies can optimize their tax position and enhance overall tax efficiency.

Finally, SPVs can be used for asset management purposes. Investors may establish SPVs to pool their capital and invest in a specific project, asset class, or geographic region. This allows investors to diversify their investment portfolio and access opportunities that may not be available through traditional investment vehicles. SPVs provide a flexible and customizable structure for managing assets and pursuing investment strategies tailored to the needs and objectives of investors.

Structure of SPVs

The structure of an SPV typically involves several key elements. First, SPVs are established as separate legal entities, distinct from the sponsoring company. This separation is essential for achieving the desired risk isolation and legal protection. SPVs are typically structured as corporations, limited liability companies (LLCs), or trusts, depending on the jurisdiction and specific requirements of the transaction.

Second, SPVs are established for a limited purpose or transaction. The purpose of the SPV is often outlined in detail in the governing documents of the entity, such as the articles of incorporation or operating agreement. This limited purpose ensures that the SPV is focused on achieving specific objectives and prevents it from engaging in activities outside the scope of its intended purpose.

Third, SPVs are designed to ring-fence the assets and liabilities associated with the transaction. This ring-fencing mechanism segregates the assets and liabilities held by the SPV from the balance sheet of the sponsoring company, protecting other assets from potential risks or losses. This separation of assets and liabilities is critical for achieving risk isolation and providing legal clarity for investors and creditors.

Finally, SPVs typically have their own independent management structure, such as a board of directors or managers. This independent management ensures that the SPV is operated in accordance with its stated purpose and objectives, providing oversight and accountability for the entity's activities. The management of the SPV is responsible for making decisions related to the operation, administration, and governance of the entity, ensuring compliance with legal and regulatory requirements, and protecting the interests of stakeholders.

Benefits and Considerations

Benefits of SPVs

Several benefits accrue to companies that utilize SPVs in their financial transactions. First and foremost, SPVs provide a mechanism for managing and mitigating financial risk. By isolating specific assets or liabilities from the sponsoring company's balance sheet, SPVs protect other assets from potential losses, enhancing overall risk management and stability.

Second, SPVs offer financial flexibility by enabling companies to raise capital, access financing, or engage in transactions without directly impacting their own creditworthiness or financial position. This financial flexibility allows companies to pursue strategic opportunities and transactions that may not be feasible through traditional financing channels.

Third, SPVs can be structured to achieve specific tax benefits, such as minimizing tax liabilities or accessing favorable tax treatment for certain types of transactions. By optimizing their tax position through the use of SPVs, companies can reduce their overall tax burden and enhance their after-tax returns on investment.

Finally, SPVs facilitate access to capital markets by enabling companies to securitize assets, issue debt or equity securities, and raise funds from investors without directly exposing their own balance sheet to the associated risks. This access to capital markets provides companies with additional sources of funding and liquidity, enabling them to pursue growth opportunities and strategic initiatives more effectively.

Considerations for Using SPVs

While SPVs offer numerous benefits, companies must also consider several key considerations when utilizing these entities in their financial transactions. First, companies must ensure compliance with legal and regulatory requirements when establishing and operating SPVs. Depending on the jurisdiction and specific characteristics of the transaction, SPVs may be subject to various laws and regulations governing corporate governance, tax, accounting, and securities.

Second, SPV structures can be complex, involving multiple parties, legal entities, and contractual arrangements. Companies must carefully plan and execute their SPV transactions to minimize complexity and ensure that all parties understand their rights, obligations, and responsibilities. Failure to properly structure and document SPV transactions can result in legal and operational challenges, including disputes, regulatory scrutiny, and reputational damage.

Third, companies must consider the implications of SPV transactions on their financial reporting and disclosure obligations. Depending on the nature of the transaction and the accounting treatment applied, companies may be required to disclose information about their SPV activities in their financial statements and regulatory filings. Companies must carefully assess these reporting and disclosure requirements and ensure compliance with applicable accounting standards and regulatory guidelines.

Finally, companies must be mindful of the potential risks associated with SPV transactions, including legal, regulatory, and operational risks. While SPVs are designed to ring-fence specific assets or liabilities, they may still be exposed to counterparty risk, credit risk, market risk, and operational risk. Companies must carefully assess and manage these risks when establishing and operating SPVs, implementing appropriate risk management strategies and controls to mitigate potential exposures.

Conclusion

Special Purpose Vehicles (SPVs) play a crucial role in a wide range of financial transactions, offering companies a flexible and efficient way to achieve specific objectives. By understanding the purpose, structure, benefits, and considerations of SPVs, companies can leverage these entities to achieve their strategic objectives, manage financial risk, and access capital markets more effectively. However, companies must also be mindful of the legal, regulatory, and operational complexities associated with SPVs and ensure that their SPV transactions are structured and executed in compliance with applicable laws and regulations. Through careful planning, execution, and ongoing management, companies can harness the benefits of SPVs while effectively managing the associated risks and challenges.

Chapter 17: Data Rooms and Documentation

Data rooms and documentation play a critical role in the due diligence process of mergers and acquisitions (M&A) and other complex transactions. This chapter explores the importance of data rooms, how to set them up and manage them effectively, and best practices for organizing and securing documentation.

Setting Up and Managing Data Rooms
Importance of Data Rooms

Data rooms serve as the nerve center of due diligence in mergers and acquisitions (M&A) and other complex transactions. In today's digital age, where information is a prized asset, data rooms provide a secure and centralized platform for sharing confidential documents and facilitating collaboration among stakeholders. They play a crucial role in enabling potential buyers, investors, and other parties to conduct thorough assessments of a target company's operations, financial health, legal standing, and other pertinent aspects before finalizing a deal.

Data rooms are particularly vital in M&A transactions, where the buyer needs access to comprehensive and up-to-date information about the target company to make informed decisions. Without a well-organized and efficiently managed data room, the due diligence process can become cumbersome, time-consuming, and prone to errors. Therefore, establishing a robust data room is essential for streamlining due diligence efforts, minimizing risks, and ensuring a smooth transaction process.

Steps for Setting Up Data Rooms

1. **Define Objectives**: Before setting up a data room, it's crucial to define the objectives of the transaction and identify the specific information required for due diligence. This involves understanding the buyer's needs, clarifying the scope of due diligence, and determining the key documents and data points that need to be included in the data room.

2. **Select a Platform**: Choosing the right platform for hosting the data room is essential for ensuring security, accessibility, and ease of use. There are numerous virtual data room (VDR) providers available, offering a range of features such as document encryption, access controls, activity tracking, and user-friendly interfaces. Carefully evaluate different platforms to select one that aligns with your organization's needs and preferences.
3. **Gather Documentation**: Collecting and organizing all relevant documentation and information is a critical step in setting up the data room. This may include financial statements, legal contracts, intellectual property records, employee information, regulatory filings, and any other documents pertinent to the transaction. Ensure that the documents are accurate, complete, and up-to-date before uploading them to the data room.
4. **Organize Information**: Structuring the data room in a logical and intuitive manner is essential for facilitating easy navigation and efficient access to information. Organize documents into categorized folders or sections based on their subject matter, departmental relevance, or transaction phase. Consider creating an index or table of contents to provide users with an overview of the contents and facilitate quick searches.
5. **Establish Access Controls**: Implementing robust access controls is crucial for safeguarding sensitive information and controlling user permissions within the data room. Determine who should have access to the data room and what level of access they require (e.g., view-only, download, edit). Assign user roles and permissions accordingly, and regularly review and update access rights as needed to ensure data security.
6. **Train Users**: Providing training and guidance to users on how to navigate the data room effectively is essential for maximizing its utility and ensuring a smooth due diligence process. Offer user training sessions or provide written instructions and tutorials to familiarize users with the data room platform, access controls, and document management features. Address any questions or concerns raised by users

and offer ongoing support throughout the due diligence process.

Managing Data Rooms Effectively

1. **Regular Updates**: Keeping the data room up to date with the latest information and documentation is essential for ensuring the accuracy and relevance of the due diligence materials. Regularly review and update the contents of the data room as new documents become available, existing documents are revised, or transaction-related developments occur. Communicate any updates or changes to users promptly to keep them informed.
2. **Monitor Activity**: Monitoring user activity within the data room provides valuable insights into the due diligence process and helps track the progress of individual users and teams. Use activity tracking features provided by the data room platform to monitor document views, downloads, edits, and other user interactions. Analyze user activity reports to identify patterns, trends, and areas of interest or concern, and use this information to guide your due diligence efforts.
3. **Address Queries**: Being responsive to queries and requests for additional information from users is essential for maintaining transparency and fostering productive communication within the data room. Promptly address any questions, concerns, or requests for clarification raised by users, and provide thorough and accurate responses to ensure that users have the information they need to conduct their due diligence effectively. Establish clear channels of communication for submitting queries and designate point persons or teams responsible for addressing them in a timely manner.
4. **Maintain Confidentiality**: Maintaining strict confidentiality and security protocols is paramount for protecting sensitive information contained within the data room. Implement robust encryption protocols to secure data both in transit and at rest, and enforce access controls to restrict access to confidential documents based on user roles and permissions. Regularly monitor user activity and audit trails to detect any

unauthorized access or suspicious behavior, and take immediate action to address security breaches or violations.

Organizing and Securing Documentation

Organizing Documentation

1. **Categorization**: Organizing documentation into logical categories or folders based on their subject matter or departmental relevance helps users quickly locate specific documents and navigate the data room efficiently. Consider grouping documents by topic, transaction phase, document type, or functional area to create a clear and intuitive folder structure. Use descriptive folder names and labels to make it easy for users to understand the contents of each folder at a glance.
2. **Indexing**: Creating an index or table of contents provides users with an overview of the documents available in the data room and facilitates quick searches. Include brief descriptions or summaries of each document to help users understand their contents and relevance to the transaction. Organize the index in a hierarchical manner, with main categories or sections followed by subcategories or subfolders, to enhance readability and usability.
3. **Version Control**: Maintaining version control for documents is essential for ensuring that users access the most recent and accurate information during the due diligence process. Clearly label documents with version numbers or dates to indicate their status and update history, and archive outdated versions as needed to prevent confusion. Consider implementing a document management system or version control software to automate version tracking and streamline document management.

Securing Documentation

1. **Encryption**: Encrypting sensitive documents helps protect them from unauthorized access or interception and ensures data security both in transit and at rest. Use encryption protocols such as Secure Sockets Layer (SSL) or Transport

Layer Security (TLS) to encrypt data transmitted over the internet, and encrypt files stored on the data room server using strong encryption algorithms. Implement multi-factor authentication (MFA) to add an extra layer of security and verify the identity of users accessing the data room.

2. **Access Controls**: Implementing access controls is essential for controlling user access to confidential information and preventing unauthorized disclosure or misuse of sensitive documents. Define user roles and permissions based on the principle of least privilege, granting access only to those users who require it to perform their job functions. Use granular access controls to specify which folders or documents each user can access and what actions they can perform (e.g., view, download, edit).

3. **Watermarking**: Applying watermarks or other visual identifiers to documents helps deter unauthorized copying, distribution, or misuse of confidential information. Watermarking adds a layer of traceability and accountability by visibly marking documents with unique identifiers such as user names, timestamps, or transaction identifiers. Use dynamic watermarks that are dynamically generated based on user-specific information to further enhance security and deter unauthorized sharing or reproduction of documents.

4. **Audit Trails**: Maintaining detailed audit trails that track user activity within the data room is essential for monitoring access, detecting unauthorized behavior, and ensuring accountability. Audit trails record key information such as user logins, document views, downloads, edits, and other user interactions, providing a comprehensive record of user activity and document access. Regularly review and analyze audit trail reports to identify any suspicious or anomalous behavior, such as unauthorized access attempts or unusual patterns of document activity, and take appropriate action to address security breaches or compliance violations.

5. **Retention Policies**: Implementing retention policies helps manage document lifecycle and ensures compliance with legal and regulatory requirements. Define clear guidelines for document retention, specifying how long documents should

be retained in the data room and when they should be archived or deleted. Consider factors such as regulatory retention requirements, business needs, and data privacy considerations when establishing retention policies. Regularly review and update retention policies to reflect changes in regulations, business practices, or transaction requirements.
6. **Data Backup and Disaster Recovery**: Implementing robust data backup and disaster recovery procedures helps safeguard against data loss, system failures, or other unforeseen events that could compromise the integrity and availability of documents stored in the data room. Regularly back up data stored in the data room to secure off-site locations or cloud storage providers, and test backup and recovery processes regularly to ensure their effectiveness. Establish contingency plans and protocols for responding to data breaches, system outages, or other emergencies, and communicate these plans to relevant stakeholders to ensure a coordinated response.
7. **User Training and Awareness**: Providing comprehensive training and awareness programs for data room users is essential for promoting best practices, enhancing security awareness, and minimizing the risk of human error or negligence. Offer training sessions, workshops, or online tutorials to educate users on data room policies, access controls, document handling procedures, and security protocols. Emphasize the importance of data security, confidentiality, and compliance with data room guidelines, and encourage users to report any security incidents or suspicious activity promptly.

By effectively setting up, managing, and securing data rooms, organizations can streamline the due diligence process, enhance collaboration among stakeholders, and mitigate risks associated with sharing sensitive information. A well-organized and securely managed data room instills confidence in potential buyers, investors, and other parties, demonstrating the organization's commitment to transparency, data security, and compliance with regulatory requirements. As data rooms continue to play a critical role in facilitating complex transactions, organizations must prioritize data room management and security to ensure successful outcomes and protect their interests.

Chapter 18: Additional Considerations

In addition to the core aspects of mergers and acquisitions (M&A) discussed in earlier chapters, there are several additional considerations that buyers and sellers must take into account to ensure a successful transaction. This chapter explores three key areas: tax implications and strategies, regulatory compliance, and risk management.

Tax Implications and Strategies
Importance of Tax Planning

Tax planning is a critical aspect of mergers and acquisitions (M&A) that can significantly impact the financial outcomes for both buyers and sellers. Proper tax planning aims to minimize tax liabilities, optimize tax efficiency, and ensure compliance with relevant tax laws and regulations. By strategically structuring the transaction and implementing tax optimization strategies, parties can maximize after-tax returns and enhance the overall value of the deal.

One of the primary objectives of tax planning in M&A is to identify and leverage tax-saving opportunities while mitigating potential tax risks. This involves analyzing the tax implications of different transaction structures, such as asset purchases, stock purchases, or mergers, and choosing the most tax-efficient option based on the specific circumstances of the transaction. Additionally, tax planning encompasses conducting thorough tax due diligence to identify potential tax exposures, such as unrecognized tax liabilities, tax disputes, or unfavorable tax positions, and developing strategies to address them effectively.

Key Tax Considerations

1. **Structuring the Transaction**: The structure of the transaction has significant tax implications for both buyers and sellers. For example, an asset purchase may allow the buyer to allocate the purchase price to specific assets, resulting in higher tax benefits through depreciation or

amortization deductions. On the other hand, a stock purchase may result in a step-up in the tax basis of the acquired assets, potentially reducing future taxable gains. By carefully evaluating the tax consequences of different transaction structures, parties can choose the structure that maximizes tax efficiency and aligns with their financial objectives.

2. **Tax Due Diligence**: Conducting comprehensive tax due diligence is essential to identify potential tax risks and opportunities associated with the target company. This involves reviewing the target company's tax compliance history, tax filings, tax positions, and any ongoing or potential tax disputes or controversies. By understanding the target company's tax profile, including its historical tax liabilities, effective tax rate, and potential tax exposures, buyers can assess the impact of tax risks on the transaction and develop strategies to mitigate them proactively.

3. **Tax Optimization Strategies**: Implementing tax optimization strategies can help minimize tax liabilities and maximize after-tax returns for both buyers and sellers. This may involve utilizing available tax credits, deductions, and incentives, structuring the transaction to optimize tax outcomes, and exploring tax-efficient exit strategies. For example, sellers may consider structuring the deal as an installment sale or utilizing tax-deferred exchange mechanisms to defer recognition of taxable gains. Similarly, buyers may explore options such as tax-free reorganizations or tax-efficient financing structures to minimize tax liabilities and enhance returns on investment.

4. **Cross-Border Tax Considerations**: In cross-border M&A transactions, navigating international tax laws and regulations is paramount. This includes considerations such as withholding taxes, transfer pricing rules, tax treaties, and foreign tax credits, which can significantly impact the tax treatment of cross-border transactions. By understanding the tax implications of operating in multiple jurisdictions and coordinating tax planning efforts across borders, parties can optimize tax outcomes, mitigate double taxation, and ensure compliance with relevant tax laws and regulations.

Regulatory Compliance
Regulatory Landscape

Navigating regulatory compliance requirements is essential in M&A transactions to mitigate legal risks, ensure regulatory approval, and maintain compliance with applicable laws and regulations. Depending on the nature of the transaction and the industries involved, various regulatory bodies may have jurisdiction over the transaction and impose specific compliance requirements.

Key Regulatory Considerations

1. **Antitrust and Competition Laws**: Compliance with antitrust and competition laws is critical to prevent anti-competitive behavior and ensure fair competition in the marketplace. Mergers and acquisitions that result in a significant market share or concentration may require approval from antitrust authorities to ensure compliance with competition regulations. Conducting thorough antitrust due diligence and obtaining necessary regulatory approvals are essential steps in ensuring regulatory compliance in M&A transactions.
2. **Securities Regulations**: Compliance with securities regulations is essential in transactions involving the issuance of securities, such as stock acquisitions or public offerings. Securities laws govern the offer, sale, and trading of securities and impose disclosure requirements, registration obligations, and other regulatory requirements on companies engaging in M&A transactions. It's essential to consult legal advisors with expertise in securities law to ensure compliance with applicable regulations and avoid potential legal pitfalls.
3. **Foreign Investment Regulations**: In cross-border M&A transactions, compliance with foreign investment regulations is essential to navigate legal and regulatory requirements in foreign jurisdictions. Many countries have specific laws and regulations governing foreign investment, including restrictions on foreign ownership, approval processes for foreign acquisitions, and national security considerations. It's essential to conduct thorough research and due diligence to

understand the foreign investment regulations applicable to the transaction and obtain any necessary approvals or clearances from regulatory authorities.
4. **Data Privacy and Cybersecurity Regulations**: Compliance with data privacy and cybersecurity regulations is increasingly important in M&A transactions, particularly in industries that handle sensitive or personal data. Data privacy laws, such as the General Data Protection Regulation (GDPR) in the European Union and the California Consumer Privacy Act (CCPA) in the United States, impose strict requirements on the collection, processing, and transfer of personal data. It's essential to assess the target company's data privacy and cybersecurity practices, identify any compliance gaps or risks, and develop strategies to address them effectively.

Risk Management

Importance of Risk Management

Risk management is fundamental in M&A transactions to identify, assess, and mitigate risks that could impact the success of the transaction. Effective risk management helps parties anticipate potential challenges, protect their interests, and make informed decisions throughout the transaction process.

Key Risk Management Considerations

1. **Financial Risk**: Financial risk encompasses various factors that could affect the financial performance and viability of the transaction. This includes risks related to market volatility, economic downturns, currency fluctuations, interest rate changes, and liquidity constraints. Conducting thorough financial due diligence and implementing financial risk mitigation strategies, such as hedging, diversification, and contingency planning, are essential to manage financial risks effectively.
2. **Legal and Regulatory Risk**: Legal and regulatory risks arise from non-compliance with applicable laws, regulations, and contractual obligations. This includes risks related to

litigation, regulatory enforcement actions, contractual breaches, intellectual property disputes, and environmental liabilities. Conducting comprehensive legal due diligence, engaging legal advisors, and implementing robust compliance programs are essential to identify, mitigate, and manage legal and regulatory risks effectively.
3. **Operational Risk**: Operational risk stems from factors that could disrupt the target company's operations or impact its ability to deliver products or services effectively. This includes risks related to supply chain disruptions, technology failures, labor disputes, cybersecurity breaches, and natural disasters. Conducting operational due diligence, assessing the target company's operational resilience, and implementing risk mitigation measures, such as business continuity planning and operational controls, are essential to manage operational risks effectively.
4. **Reputational Risk**: Reputational risk arises from negative publicity, public perception, or stakeholder reactions that could damage the reputation and credibility of the parties involved in the transaction. This includes risks related to ethical misconduct, corporate governance failures, customer complaints, and social responsibility issues. Implementing robust corporate governance practices, maintaining transparency and accountability, and proactively addressing reputational concerns are essential to protect against reputational risk and preserve stakeholder trust and confidence.

By addressing tax implications and strategies, regulatory compliance, and risk management considerations proactively, parties can mitigate legal, financial, and operational risks, enhance transaction certainty, and maximize the likelihood of a successful outcome. Collaboration with experienced advisors, including tax professionals, legal counsel, and risk management experts, is essential to navigate the complexities of M&A transactions effectively and achieve the desired objectives while minimizing potential pitfalls and challenges.

Tax Implications and Strategies
Cross-Border Tax Considerations

In cross-border M&A transactions, navigating international tax laws and regulations is crucial. Several factors come into play, including:

1. **Withholding Taxes**: Different jurisdictions may impose withholding taxes on cross-border transactions, such as dividends, interest, or royalties. Understanding the applicable withholding tax rates and any available exemptions or reduced rates under tax treaties is essential for optimizing tax outcomes.
2. **Transfer Pricing Rules**: Transfer pricing regulations govern the pricing of transactions between related parties in different tax jurisdictions. Compliance with transfer pricing rules requires ensuring that transactions are conducted at arm's length prices, reflecting market conditions. Failure to comply with transfer pricing regulations can result in tax adjustments, penalties, and disputes with tax authorities.
3. **Tax Treaties**: Many countries have tax treaties in place to prevent double taxation and promote cross-border trade and investment. Tax treaties typically provide rules for allocating taxing rights between treaty countries and may offer benefits such as reduced withholding tax rates on certain types of income. Understanding the provisions of relevant tax treaties and leveraging treaty benefits can help minimize tax liabilities in cross-border transactions.
4. **Foreign Tax Credits**: Taxpayers may be entitled to claim foreign tax credits for taxes paid to foreign jurisdictions on income earned abroad. Foreign tax credits can help mitigate the impact of double taxation and reduce the overall tax burden on cross-border transactions. However, claiming foreign tax credits requires compliance with specific documentation and reporting requirements under domestic tax laws.

Regulatory Compliance
Data Privacy and Cybersecurity Regulations

Data privacy and cybersecurity regulations are increasingly stringent worldwide, imposing strict requirements on companies that handle sensitive or personal data. Key considerations include:

1. **Compliance Obligations**: Companies must comply with data privacy laws and regulations applicable to their operations, such as the GDPR in the EU, the CCPA in California, and similar laws in other jurisdictions. Compliance obligations may include obtaining consent for data processing, implementing data security measures, and providing individuals with rights to access, correct, or delete their personal data.
2. **Data Protection Impact Assessments (DPIAs)**: DPIAs are systematic assessments of the potential impact of data processing activities on individuals' privacy rights. Conducting DPIAs helps identify and mitigate privacy risks associated with data processing activities, ensuring compliance with data privacy regulations and enhancing data protection measures.
3. **Data Breach Notification Requirements**: Data privacy laws often require companies to notify regulators and affected individuals in the event of a data breach involving personal data. Promptly reporting data breaches and taking appropriate remedial actions are essential for complying with breach notification requirements and mitigating the impact of data breaches on affected individuals and organizations.
4. **Cybersecurity Measures**: Implementing robust cybersecurity measures is critical for protecting against data breaches, unauthorized access, and other cybersecurity threats. This may include implementing firewalls, encryption, access controls, and security monitoring systems to safeguard sensitive data and prevent unauthorized access or disclosure.

Risk Management
Reputational Risk Management

Reputational risk management is essential for preserving the trust and confidence of stakeholders and maintaining a positive corporate image. Key considerations include:

1. **Crisis Management Planning**: Developing crisis management plans and protocols for responding to reputational crises, such as scandals, adverse publicity, or social media controversies. Effective crisis management involves identifying potential reputational risks, implementing proactive measures to mitigate them, and responding promptly and transparently to crisis situations to protect the organization's reputation.
2. **Stakeholder Communication**: Maintaining open and transparent communication with stakeholders, including employees, customers, investors, and the media, is essential for managing reputational risks effectively. Providing timely updates, addressing concerns, and demonstrating a commitment to ethical conduct and corporate responsibility can help build trust and credibility with stakeholders and mitigate the impact of negative publicity or reputational challenges.
3. **Brand Monitoring and Analysis**: Monitoring online and offline channels for mentions, discussions, and sentiment related to the organization's brand is critical for identifying potential reputational risks and addressing them proactively. By analyzing brand mentions, social media conversations, and media coverage, organizations can gain insights into public perceptions, identify emerging issues, and take corrective actions to protect their reputation.
4. **Corporate Social Responsibility (CSR)**: Demonstrating a commitment to corporate social responsibility (CSR) and sustainability initiatives can help enhance the organization's reputation and mitigate reputational risks. Engaging in socially responsible business practices, supporting community initiatives, and addressing environmental, social, and governance (ESG) issues can strengthen stakeholder trust

and goodwill, reducing the likelihood of reputational harm in the event of adverse events or controversies.

By addressing cross-border tax considerations, regulatory compliance, and reputational risk management proactively, parties can mitigate legal, financial, and reputational risks associated with M&A transactions, enhancing transaction certainty and maximizing the likelihood of a successful outcome. Collaboration with experienced advisors, including tax professionals, legal counsel, and risk management experts, is essential to navigate the complexities of M&A transactions effectively and achieve the desired objectives while minimizing potential pitfalls and challenges.

Chapter 19: Conclusion

In this comprehensive guide to mergers and acquisitions (M&A), we have explored a wide range of key concepts, strategies, and considerations essential for navigating the complex landscape of business transactions. As we conclude our journey, let's recap the key concepts and strategies covered in this book and look ahead to future opportunities in the dynamic world of M&A.

Recap of Key Concepts and Strategies

Throughout this book, we have delved into various aspects of M&A, including:

1. **Leveraged Buyouts (LBOs)**: We explored the fundamentals of leveraged buyouts, including their definition, advantages, and risks, providing insights into how LBOs are structured and executed.
2. **Mindset and Preparation**: We discussed the importance of developing the right mindset, understanding risk and reward, and assessing personal and financial readiness before embarking on M&A activities.
3. **Setting Acquisition Criteria**: We examined the process of setting acquisition criteria, including identifying target industries, defining company size and financial metrics, and considering geographic considerations.
4. **Deal Sourcing Strategies**: We explored various strategies for sourcing deals, including leveraging virtual assistants, networking, and using online platforms and resources to identify potential acquisition opportunities.
5. **Communicating with Sellers**: We discussed the importance of crafting persuasive letters and emails, establishing trust and credibility, and emphasizing safety and stability when communicating with sellers.
6. **Best Sectors to Target**: We analyzed different sectors and industries, evaluating industry trends, growth potential, and competitive landscapes to identify the best sectors for investment.

7. **Understanding Valuation Methods**: We explored valuation methods such as discounted cash flow (DCF) analysis, EBITDA and free cash flow (FCF) multiples, and comparables and market analysis to determine the fair value of target companies.
8. **Negotiating the Deal**: We discussed strategies for win-win negotiations, balancing price, terms, and conditions, and handling counteroffers and objections to secure the best deal for all parties involved.
9. **Deal Structure and Financing**: We examined different financing options, including asset-based lending, invoice financing, and merchant financing, and explored how to leverage target company assets and cash reserves to finance the deal.
10. **Positioning Yourself as a Buyer**: We explored strategies for building a strong personal brand, demonstrating expertise and experience, and creating a professional image to position yourself as a credible and desirable buyer.
11. **Heads of Terms/LOI**: We discussed the importance of understanding key terms and conditions and drafting comprehensive heads of terms or letters of intent to outline the preliminary agreement between parties.
12. **Due Diligence Process**: We examined the due diligence process, including conducting thorough financial analysis, assessing legal, regulatory, and compliance issues, and evaluating operational and strategic fit.
13. **Contract Negotiation and Drafting**: We explored the importance of working with legal professionals to negotiate and draft contracts, ensuring clarity and legal compliance throughout the transaction.
14. **Closing the Deal**: We discussed the final steps in the M&A process, including finalizing legal and financial documents and celebrating successful completion of the transaction.
15. **Post-Acquisition Management**: We examined the importance of the first 90 days post-acquisition, including integration and transition, implementing growth strategies, and monitoring performance to ensure a smooth transition and maximize value creation.

16. **Special Purpose Vehicles (SPVs)**: We explored the purpose and structure of special purpose vehicles (SPVs) and the benefits and considerations of using SPVs in M&A transactions.
17. **Data Rooms and Documentation**: We discussed setting up and managing data rooms, organizing and securing documentation, and ensuring compliance with data privacy and security regulations.
18. **Additional Considerations**: We examined tax implications and strategies, regulatory compliance, and risk management considerations, including cross-border tax considerations, data privacy and cybersecurity regulations, and reputational risk management.

Looking Ahead to Future Opportunities

As we look ahead to the future of M&A, several trends and opportunities are shaping the landscape:

1. **Technology and Innovation**: The rapid pace of technological innovation is driving M&A activity in sectors such as artificial intelligence, cybersecurity, and renewable energy, presenting opportunities for growth and investment.
2. **Cross-Border Transactions**: Globalization continues to fuel cross-border M&A activity, with companies seeking to expand their reach into new markets and access new sources of talent, technology, and capital.
3. **ESG Considerations**: Environmental, social, and governance (ESG) factors are increasingly influencing M&A decisions, with companies prioritizing sustainability, diversity, and corporate responsibility in their strategic initiatives.
4. **Industry Consolidation**: Industry consolidation is a prevalent trend in sectors such as healthcare, financial services, and technology, as companies seek to achieve economies of scale, enhance market share, and drive operational efficiencies through strategic acquisitions.
5. **Private Equity and Venture Capital**: Private equity and venture capital continue to play a significant role in driving

M&A activity, with firms deploying capital to fund acquisitions, facilitate growth, and unlock value in portfolio companies.
6. **Regulatory Environment**: Evolving regulatory frameworks, including changes in tax laws, antitrust regulations, and data privacy rules, will continue to shape the M&A landscape and influence deal structures and strategies.
7. **Geopolitical Uncertainty**: Geopolitical factors such as trade tensions, Brexit, and geopolitical conflicts can introduce volatility and uncertainty into the M&A market, impacting deal flow and investor sentiment.

In conclusion, mergers and acquisitions offer significant opportunities for growth, innovation, and value creation, but navigating the complexities of M&A requires careful planning, execution, and adaptation to changing market dynamics. By leveraging the strategies and insights provided in this book and remaining vigilant to emerging trends and opportunities, businesses can position themselves for success in the dynamic and competitive world of M&A.

Chapter 20: Partner with Epitome Capital and Leverage Our Resources

Partnering with Epitome Capital offers a strategic advantage for businesses looking to embark on mergers and acquisitions (M&A) ventures. With our extensive expertise, network of contacts, and comprehensive resources, we provide valuable support and guidance throughout the entire M&A process. Here's how partnering with Epitome Capital can benefit your M&A endeavors:

Access to Templates and Tools

We offer a wide range of templates, tools, and resources designed to streamline the M&A process and facilitate efficient deal execution. Our library includes:

- Letter of Intent (LOI) templates

- Due diligence checklists
- Contract negotiation guides
- Financial modeling templates
- Data room management tools
- Communication templates for engaging with sellers and stakeholders

These resources are meticulously crafted and continuously updated to reflect industry best practices and regulatory requirements, enabling you to navigate the complexities of M&A transactions with confidence and ease.

Extensive Network of Contacts

Our extensive network of contacts spans across industries, geographies, and sectors, providing access to a diverse pool of potential buyers, sellers, investors, and advisors. Whether you're seeking acquisition targets, financing opportunities, or strategic partners, our network enables us to connect you with the right opportunities and facilitate meaningful collaborations that drive value and growth.

Expert Guidance and Advisory Services

Our team of seasoned M&A professionals offers expert guidance and advisory services tailored to your specific needs and objectives. From strategic planning and target identification to due diligence, negotiation, and closing, we provide comprehensive support at every stage of the M&A process. Our deep industry knowledge, analytical expertise, and strategic insights empower you to make informed decisions, mitigate risks, and maximize value creation in your M&A transactions.

Strategic Partnership Opportunities

Partnering with Epitome Capital opens doors to strategic partnership opportunities that can fuel your growth and expansion initiatives. Whether you're looking to explore joint ventures, strategic alliances, or cross-border partnerships, we leverage our extensive network and industry expertise to identify and facilitate mutually beneficial collaborations that align with your strategic objectives and drive long-term value creation.

Ongoing Support and Relationship Management

Our commitment to client success extends beyond the transactional phase, as we provide ongoing support and relationship management to ensure continued success and value realization post-acquisition. We remain actively engaged with our clients, offering strategic guidance, performance monitoring, and operational support to optimize post-acquisition integration, drive growth initiatives, and maximize return on investment.

In conclusion, partnering with Epitome Capital offers a unique opportunity to leverage our expertise, resources, and network to achieve your M&A objectives effectively and efficiently. Whether you're a seasoned acquirer or embarking on your first M&A venture, our team is dedicated to helping you navigate the complexities of the M&A landscape and unlock opportunities for growth, innovation, and value creation. Contact us today to explore how we can support your M&A endeavors and propel your business to new heights of success.

www.ingramcontent.com/pod-product-compliance
Lightning Source LLC
Chambersburg PA
CBHW020438220526
45464CB00002B/758